10/97

THE BOOK OF TEA

D0050311

(Overleaf: *The making and sharing of a bowl of tea give rise to a profound aesthetic experience.*)

THE BOOK OF TEA

KAKUZO OKAKURA

Foreword and Afterword by
SOSHITSU SEN XV

KODANSHA INTERNATIONAL
Tokyo • New York • London

Foreword and Afterword: Translation by the Urasenke Foundation, Foreign Affairs Division.

Distributed in the United States by Kodansha America, Inc., 114 Fifth Avenue, New York, N.Y. 10011, and in the United Kingdom and continental Europe by Kodansha Europe Ltd., 95 Aldwych, London WC2B 4JF. Published by Kodansha International Ltd., 17-14 Otowa 1-chome, Bunkyo-ku, Tokyo 112, and Kodansha America, Inc.

ISBN 4-7700-1542-9
LCC 89-45170

First Kodansha International edition, 1989
First paperback edition, 1991
    97 98 99 10 9 8 7

CONTENTS

List of Photographs

Photographs by Takao Inoue.

FOREWORD

THE BOOK OF TEA, by Kakuzo Okakura, has served for nearly a century as one of the most perceptive introductions to Asian life and thought in English. It was a pioneering effort in the cultural bridge-building between East and West, and it remains an endeavor of note in contemporary life. If this book once startled readers with the exoticism of its subject, it continues to surprise us with the freshness of its insights and the incisiveness of its language.

Chado—literally the way of tea—or *chanoyu*—widely known as the "tea ceremony"—holds an aura of mystery for many people, but its governing impulse is simple: a small number of friends come together to spend several hours in partaking of a meal, drinking tea, and enjoying a brief respite from the busyness of daily concerns. The guests, passing through a small garden of trees and shrubbery, enter the quiet, intimate space of the tea room, which is shaded from any glaring light. In the alcove hangs a scroll, often inscribed with words of a Zen master. A few flowers are arranged in a simple manner in a vase. In this tranquillity, suggesting the atmosphere of an isolated hut, host and guests recollect themselves and, while carrying on the most ordinary activities of human life, seek to relate to each other and to all the elements of their environment with directness, immediacy, and profound appreciation.

Okakura wrote *The Book of Tea* in 1906, in English, to convey the spirit and the atmosphere of chanoyu to readers in the West. It was composed at a time when his own countrymen avidly sought to Westernize every aspect of Japanese life, and at precisely that moment in history when Japan astonished the world by defeating Russia with a modern naval power developed miraculously within the span of few decades of dedicated study.

Thirty-two years earlier, chanoyu itself had been confronted with one of its most endangering tests—the Meiji Government's decision to classify it as a "performing art." Only through the emphatic petition of Gengensai, my ancestor four generations before me, did it narrowly escape that official label. Chanoyu has since been recognized as a way of life.

It is not too much to say that Okakura and Gengensai, in

their courage and discernment, were of like mind and spirit. It is a tribute to those qualities that Okakura opposed the wholesale abandonment of traditional culture, and that he was able to see in chanoyu a cultural achievement which could be held up beside military might or industrial prowess, and which should be staunchly championed for its intrinsic worth to human life.

Okakura was in some ways an unlikely candidate for his role of introducing chanoyu to the West. Although he studied chanoyu as a youth, the house he built in Japan shows little trace of his active practice of chado in daily life. Moreover, one senses in his irony and passion, scarcely concealed by the elegance of his literary style, more fire of spirit than is usually deemed appropriate in the tea room. With characteristic self-awareness, Okakura himself confesses: "Perhaps I betray my own ignorance of the Tea Cult by being so outspoken." One senses that this is far from an apology, however, for to him his mission was clear. Other books on chanoyu already existed in English, but Okakura's purpose was distinct. Writing at the time of Japan's first success in utilizing Western military methods, Okakura took upon himself the task of interpreting Japanese civilization for the West. In writing of chanoyu, his concern was the broad current of Asian culture flowing eastward from India, and its potential contribution to the culture of all humankind. Whether it was his intent or not, by his refusing to pose as a master of chanoyu, he was perhaps the more effective as its champion.

To my mind, three elements in Okakura's early education played an important role in his conceiving of *The Book of Tea*. The first was his contact with Westerners and with Western learning. Okakura was born in 1862, as Japan was emerging from over two centuries of isolation from the rest of the world. Commodore Perry had opened Tokyo Bay to foreign ships in 1860, and it was at the nearby port of Yokohama that Okakura was born.

His father, a samurai of rank within his clan, had been sent from Fukui to the newly active port city. Although it had long been merely a fishing village, Yokohama was quickly growing into a trading center, and it seems that the Okakura store, dealing in silk thread produced in Fukui, prospered from the numerous customers from foreign lands. It was in this milieu that young Okakura began his education in the English language, and probably also in the social skills that later enabled him to move about in Boston society with such poise and confidence.

The Book of Tea gives ample testimony of Okakura's linguistic genius. The style shows such freedom of expression that one might suspect the hand of a native speaker, but we must bear in mind the eagerness of the Japanese of this period to absorb the achievements of the West. Okakura was among the students at Tokyo University when it was first established in 1877. It was an institute for Western learning, and instruction was in English, the professors invited from abroad. Even here, Okakura's mastery of English seems to have been prominent, for he often served as interpreter for instructors.

I suspect that Okakura's sweeping grasp of epochs and cultures—for example, his portrayal of the "emotional impulses" behind Chinese methods of preparing tea as classic, romantic, and naturalistic—stemmed from his training in Western thought. Time and again, his broad vision—far transcending the framework within which the traditional arts had been viewed—opened new perspectives on what lay at the foundations of Japanese culture.

The second major element of his early education was his

study of the Chinese classics. Though he began his study of English as a lad of nine under foreign tutors, Okakura did not turn his gaze solely to the West. It is said that, embarrassed at not being able to read a sign in Japanese, he resolved to take up the study of Chinese classics. This resolution, however, bore some relation as well to the loss of his mother, who fell ill and died when he was eight and whose death affected him deeply throughout his life. When his father remarried, Okakura was sent for several years to live in a Buddhist temple. There, while continuing with his English lessons, he studied the Chinese classics under the resident priest. Okakura's interest in the religious culture of the East may have developed from this period of learning, culminating in his perception of chanoyu as a form of spiritual discipline. It might be noted that, like his style in English, his writings in Japanese display a loftiness of tone that reflects his training in Chinese.

The third basic element in Okakura's education was his interest in art. He began his study of Japanese painting at the age of fourteen, about the same time that he began to participate in gatherings for reading and writing poetry in Chinese.

These various aspects of Okakura can be seen in *The Book of Tea*, but it would be fair to say that they were first brought together in Okakura's encounter with the American scholar, Ernest Fenollosa. Fenollosa, who is esteemed in Japan for his role in preserving Japanese art when it was little appreciated in its own land, joined the Tokyo University faculty as an instructor in philosophy in 1878. He was twenty-six years old, and Okakura was one of his students.

In Tokyo, Fenollosa's interest in Japanese art and architecture deepened. Accompanied by Okakura, who served as his interpreter, he frequented antique shops and galleries collecting the art of Japan. Assisted by Okakura, who translated the texts for him, he studied the literature on art. Thus prepared, Fenollosa proceeded to give a series of lectures on Japanese art, again with the help of Okakura. It was an association between the two men that continued even after Okakura's graduation. Together, they worked to urge the government to take steps to protect and preserve Japanese art, and when a commission was formed, both were employed to study and catalog art treasures in temples and shrines.

It was under Fenollosa's tutelage, then, that Okakura

first explored the riches of the heritage of Japanese art—an endeavor he pursued throughout his life. He was in his early twenties when he and Fenollosa supervised the monks of Horyuji temple in Nara in the opening of a locked shrine, revealing an important Buddhist statue that, unknown to all, had lain hidden away for two hundred years. And the preservation of wall paintings at that same temple was one of his final achievements in life.

Through Fenollosa, Okakura met several friends who would later be important figures in his life in Boston. In particular, there were William Sturgis Bigelow, who amassed the large collection of Japanese art objects that was to become the core of the Asiatic collection of the Museum of Fine Arts in Boston, and Mrs. Isabella Stewart Gardner, at whose house in Brookline, a suburb of Boston, Okakura was to deliver his first reading of *The Book of Tea*.

It is critical to note that, despite his appreciation of the ancient past, Okakura's interest in art was by no means antiquarian. His concern was "living art," whatever its period. In pursuing it into the past he journeyed to China and India, where he became convinced that "Asia is one," that the diverse cultures of Asia were unified at their roots.

At the same time, he discovered that Japan served as a treasury of art, a "museum of Asiatic civilization," with treasures from the range of history.

After graduation, while still in his twenties, Okakura held various government posts involving fine arts. He was charged with founding a government art school and also served as curator of the Imperial Museum of Fine Arts. In these posts, he actively supported young artists.

Okakura was forced to quit his government posts, partly because of an indiscretion he committed, when he was thirty-six. He then established a private art school for young art students, but as the school's vitality waned, Okakura left Japan first for India, then, in 1904, for the United States. There he accepted the position of consultant to the Chinese and Japanese department of the Museum of Fine Arts in Boston. From that time on, he remained closely associated with the museum, with frequent trips to Europe, China, India, and Japan.

It appears that during a period of rest in Japan in 1905, Okakura began formulating plans for *The Book of Tea* and gathering materials for it. Though he was familiar with the practices of tea and the atmosphere of the tea room, his aim was not to address chanoyu in its concrete aspects, but rather to give voice to traditional Asian values and ideals that had been little recognized in the West. Thus, he sought to convey the spirit of chanoyu as a crystallization of the cultural life of the East. Just as Japan served as a repository of the historical traditions of the Asian mainland, so chanoyu might be seen as the living synthesis of traditional arts.

Among the elements of Okakura's education that contributed to the comprehensiveness of his vision in *The Book of Tea*, it was his involvement with art that had become the focus. Okakura, in choosing chanoyu as a symbol for explaining the Asian concept of art, may have been following in the footsteps of the great tea masters of the past. He states that after the decline of the imperial house during the medieval period in Japan, it was the tea masters who recorded, catalogued, and worked for the preservation of the treasures of the past.

However, Okakura's experience with the West allowed him a perspective beyond the confines of any single school or tradition of chanoyu. His advocacy of aesthetic appreciation was thus able to avoid the pitfalls of elitism. In one particularly impressive passage, which casts a clear light on the practice of chanoyu, Okakura proffered how chanoyu "represents the true spirit of Eastern democracy by making all its votaries aristocrats in taste." He perceived chanoyu as a form of spiritual culture, a discipline that transforms itself into an "Art of Life." It encompasses an appreciation of the most ordinary items of daily life, and at its core lies a "moral geometry" that keeps us mindful of our place in the greater scheme of the universe. Never more than now has such an understanding been needed.

Okakura's comprehension of chanoyu, springing largely from his broad learning in Chinese, was rooted in the religious values of Buddhism, Taoism, and Confucianism. Art, in such terms, stands against all that is false, grasping, and self-serving. Okakura states: "We never forgive others because we know that we ourselves are in the wrong. We nurse a conscience because we are afraid to tell the truth to others; we take refuge in pride because we are afraid to tell the truth to ourselves." It is in nurturing aesthetic and moral sensitivity that human beings can approach that which is true and authentic in their existence, and chanoyu has evolved as a path to such a life.

In groping for a suitable expression for this dimension of chanoyu, Okakura speaks of "Teaism," or the "Tea Cult." Neither of these terms is adequate, and neither has entered common usage, for though they convey the religious element in the way of tea, they place it in a Western dimension. Chanoyu, as Okakura explains, remains embedded in concrete practice, and in the living appreciation of beauty in ordinary things. While many people have always sought to erect imposing and lasting monuments to human greatness, Okakura resisted the headlong drive of his times toward industrialization and militarism, and, with boldness and imagination, composed a small book that, embodying the spirit of a tea gathering, continues to refresh us and remind us of our humanity today.

The Book of Tea hence remains a remarkably valuable essay, not only for what it tells us about the state of American understanding of Japan at the turn of the twentieth century, but also for its reminder, no less valid today, that the beauty of flowers is not less essential to human existence than the latest convenience or material comfort, but more. In this respect, it is a classic in the genuine sense, being firmly rooted in its own milieu, and at the same time transcending its time and setting.

At the close of his book, Okakura presents a splendid evocation of the death of Sen Rikyu, the tea master who brought chanoyu to its highest development and whose heritage I am proud to succeed now fifteen generations later. Death, says Okakura, must not be shunned as mere negation of life; "he only who has lived with the beautiful can die beautifully." It is now four hundred years since the death of Rikyu, and as we reflect on the course of chanoyu down through history, and into the twenty-first century, it is fitting that we turn once more to *The Book of Tea*.

Soshitsu Sen XV

Kyoto
October 1989

THE BOOK OF TEA

(Overleaf: *The suffusion of powdered tea and hot water serves as a spiritual elixir.*)

THE CUP OF HUMANITY

TEA BEGAN as a medicine and grew into a beverage. In China, in the eighth century, it entered the realm of poetry as one of the polite amusements. The fifteenth century saw Japan ennoble it into a religion of aestheticism—Teaism. Teaism is a cult founded on the adoration of the beautiful among the sordid facts of everyday existence. It inculcates purity and harmony, the mystery of mutual charity, the romanticism of the social order. It is essentially a worship of the Imperfect, as it is a tender attempt to accomplish something possible in this impossible thing we know as life.

The Philosophy of Tea is not mere aestheticism in the ordinary acceptance of the term, for it expresses conjointly with ethics and religion our whole point of view about man and nature. It is hygiene, for it enforces cleanliness; it is economics, for it shows comfort in simplicity rather than in the complex and costly; it is moral geometry, inasmuch as it defines our sense of proportion to the universe. It represents the true spirit of Eastern democracy by making all its votaries aristocrats in taste.

The long isolation of Japan from the rest of the world, so conducive to introspection, has been highly favourable to the development of Teaism. Our home and habits, costume and cuisine, porcelain, lacquer, painting—our very literature—all have been subject to its influence. No student of Japanese culture could ever ignore its presence. It has permeated the elegance of noble boudoirs, and entered the abode of the humble. Our peasants have learned to arrange flowers, our meanest labourer to offer his salutation to the rocks and waters. In our common parlance we speak of the man "with no tea" in him, when he is insusceptible to the serio-comic interests of the personal drama. Again we stigmatise the untamed aesthete who, regardless of the mundane tragedy, runs riot in the springtide of emancipated emotions, as one "with too much tea" in him.

The outsider may indeed wonder at this seeming much ado about nothing. What a tempest in a tea-cup! he will say. But when we consider how small after all the cup of human enjoyment is, how soon overflowed with tears, how easily drained to the dregs in our quenchless thirst for infinity, we shall not blame ourselves for making so much of the tea-cup. Mankind has done worse. In the worship of Bacchus, we have sacrificed too freely; and we have even transfigured the gory image of Mars. Why not consecrate ourselves to the queen of the Camellias, and revel in the warm stream of sympathy that flows from her altar? In the liquid amber within the ivory-porcelain, the initiated may touch the sweet reticence of Confucius, the piquancy of Laotse, and the ethereal aroma of Sakyamuni himself.

Those who cannot feel the littleness of great things in themselves are apt to overlook the greatness of little things in others. The average Westerner, in his sleek complacency, will see in the tea-ceremony but another instance of the thousand and one oddities which constitute the quaintness and childishness of the East to him. He was wont to regard Japan as barbarous while she indulged in the gentle arts of peace: he calls her civilised since she began to commit wholesale slaughter on Manchurian battlefields. Much comment has been given lately to the Code of the Samurai—the Art of Death which makes our soldiers exult in self-sacrifice; but scarcely any attention has been drawn to Teaism, which represents so much of our Art of Life. Fain would we remain barbarians, if our claim to civilisation were to be based on the gruesome glory of war. Fain would we await the time when due respect shall be paid to our art and ideals.

When will the West understand, or try to understand, the East? We Asiatics are often appalled by the curious web of facts and fancies which has been woven concerning us. We are pictured as living on the perfume of the lotus, if not on mice and cockroaches. It is either impotent fanaticism or else abject voluptuousness. Indian spirituality has been derided as ignorance, Chinese sobriety as stupidity, Japanese patriotism as the result of fatalism. It has been said that we are less sensible to pain and wounds on account of the callousness of our nervous organisation!

Why not amuse yourselves at our expense? Asia returns the compliment. There would be further food for merriment if you were to know all that we have imagined and written about you. All the glamour of the perspective is there, all the unconscious homage of wonder, all the silent resentment of the new and undefined. You have been loaded with virtues too refined to be envied, and accused of crimes too picturesque to be condemned. Our writers in the past—the wise men who knew—informed us that you had bushy tails somewhere hidden in your garments, and often dined off a fricassee of newborn babes! Nay, we had something worse against you: we used to think you the most impracticable people on the earth, for you were said to preach what you never practised.

Such misconceptions are fast vanishing amongst us. Commerce has forced the European tongues on many an Eastern port. Asiatic youths are flocking to Western colleges for the equipment of modern education. Our insight does not penetrate your culture deeply, but at least we are willing to learn. Some of my compatriots have adopted too much of your customs and too much of your etiquette, in the delusion that the acquisition of stiff collars and tall silk hats comprised the attainment of your civilisation. Pathetic and deplorable as such affectations are, they evince our willingness to approach the West on our knees. Unfortunately the Western attitude is unfavourable to the understanding of the East. The Christian missionary goes to impart, but not to receive. Your information is based on the meagre translations of our immense literature, if not on the unreliable anecdotes of passing travellers. It is rarely that the chivalrous pen of a Lafcadio Hearn or that of the author of "The Web of Indian Life" enlivens the Oriental darkness with the torch of our own sentiments.

Perhaps I betray my own ignorance of the Tea Cult by being so outspoken. Its very spirit of politeness exacts that you say what you are expected to say, and no more. But I am not to be a polite Teaist. So much harm has been done already by the mutual misunderstanding of the New World and the Old, that one need not apologise for contributing his tithe to the furtherance of a better understanding. The beginning of the twentieth century would have been spared the spectacle of sanguinary warfare if Russia had condescended to know Japan better. What dire consequences to humanity lie in the contemptuous ignoring of Eastern problems! European imperialism, which does not disdain to raise the absurd cry of the Yellow Peril, fails to realise that Aisa may also awaken to the cruel sense of the White Disaster. You may laugh at us for having "too much tea," but may we not suspect that you of the West have "no tea" in your constitution?

Let us stop the continents from hurling epigrams at each other, and be sadder if not wiser by the mutual gain of half a hemisphere. We have developed along different lines, but there is no reason why one should not supplement the other. You have gained expansion at the cost of restlessness; we have created a harmony which is weak against aggression. Will you believe it?—the East is better off in some respects than the West!

Strangely enough humanity has so far met in the teacup. It is the only Asiatic ceremonial which commands universal esteem. The white man has scoffed at our religion and our morals, but has accepted the brown beverage without hesitation. The afternoon tea is now an important function in Western society. In the delicate clatter of trays and saucers, in the soft rustle of feminine hospitality, in the common catechism about cream and sugar, we know that the Worship of Tea is established beyond question. The philosophic resignation of the guest to the fate awaiting him in the dubious decoction proclaims that in this single instance the Oriental spirit reigns supreme.

The earliest record of tea in European writing is said to be found in the statement of an Arabian traveller, that after the year 879 the main sources of revenue in Canton were the duties on salt and tea. Marco Polo records the deposition of a Chinese minister of finance in 1285 for his arbitrary augmentation of the tea-taxes. It was at the period of the great discoveries that the European people began to know more about the extreme Orient. At the end of the sixteenth century the Hollanders brought the news that a pleasant drink was made in the East from the leaves of a bush. The travellers Giovanni Batista Ramusio (1559), L. Almeida (1576), Maffeno (1588), Tareira (1610), also mentioned tea. In the last-named year ships of the Dutch East India Company brought the first tea into Europe. It was known in France in 1636, and reached Russia in 1638. England welcomed it in 1650 and spoke of it as "that excellent and by all physicians approved China drink, called by the Chineans Tcha, and by other nations Tay, alias Tee."

Like all the good things of the world, the propaganda of Tea met with opposition. Heretics like Henry Saville (1678) denounced drinking it as a filthy custom. Jonas Hanway (Essay on Tea, 1756) said that men seemed to lose their stature and comeliness, women their beauty through the use of tea. Its cost at the start (about fifteen or sixteen shillings a pound) forbade popular consumption, and made it "regalia for high treatments and entertainments, presents being made thereof to princes and grandees." Yet in spite of such drawbacks tea-drinking spread with marvellous rapidity. The coffee-houses of London in the early half of the eighteenth century became, in fact, tea-houses, the resort of wits like Addison and Steele, who beguiled themselves over their "dish of tea." The beverage soon became a necessary of life—a taxable matter. We are reminded in this connection what an important part it plays in modern history. Colonial America resigned herself to oppression until human endurance gave way before the heavy duties laid on Tea. American independence dates from the throwing of tea-chests into Boston harbour.

There is a subtle charm in the taste of tea which makes it irresistible and capable of idealisation. Western humourists were not slow to mingle the fragrance of their thought with its aroma. It has not the arrogance of wine, the self-consciousness of coffee, nor the simpering innocence of cocoa. Already in 1711, says the Spectator: "I would therefore in a particular manner recommend these my speculations to all well-regulated families that set apart an hour every morning for tea, bread and butter; and would earnestly advise them for their good to order this paper to be punctually served up and to be looked upon as a part of the tea-equipage." Samuel Johnson draws his own portrait as "a hardened and shameless tea-drinker, who for twenty years diluted his meals with only the infusion of the fascinating plant; who with tea amused the evening, with tea solaced the midnight, and with tea welcomed the morning."

Charles Lamb, a professed devotee, sounded the true note of Teaism when he wrote that the greatest pleasure he knew was to do a good action by stealth, and to have it found out by accident. For Teaism is the art of concealing beauty that you may discover it, of suggesting what you dare not reveal. It is the noble secret of laughing at yourself, calmly yet thoroughly, and is thus humour itself—the smile of philosophy. All genuine humourists may in this sense be called tea-philosophers—Thackeray, for instance, and, of course, Shakespeare. The poets of the Decadence (when was not the world in decadence?), in their protests against materialism, have, to a certain extent, also opened the way to Teaism. Perhaps nowadays it is in our demure contemplation of the Imperfect that the West and the East can meet in mutual consolation.

The Taoists relate that at the great beginning of the No-Beginning, Spirit and Matter met in mortal combat. At last the Yellow Emperor, the Sun of Heaven, triumphed over Shuhyung, the demon of darkness and earth. The Titan, in his death agony, struck his head against the solar vault and shivered the blue dome of jade into fragments. The stars lost their nests, the moon wandered aimlessly among the wild chasms of the night. In despair the Yellow Emperor sought far and wide for the repairer of the Heavens. He had not to search in vain. Out of the Eastern sea rose a queen, the divine Niuka, horn-crowned and dragon-tailed, resplendent in her armour of fire. She welded the five-coloured rainbow in her magic cauldron and rebuilt the Chinese sky. But it is also told that Niuka forgot to fill two tiny crevices in the blue firmament. Thus began the dualism of love—two souls rolling through space and never at rest until they join together to complete the universe. Everyone has to build anew his sky of hope and peace.

The heaven of modern humanity is indeed shattered in the Cyclopean struggle for wealth and power. The world is groping in the shadow of egotism and vulgarity. Knowledge is bought through a bad conscience, benevolence practised for the sake of utility. The East and West, like two dragons tossed in a sea of ferment, in vain strive to regain the jewel of life. We need a Niuka again to repair the grand devastation; we await the great Avatar. Meanwhile, let us have a sip of tea. The afternoon glow is brightening the bamboos, the fountains are bubbling with delight, the soughing of the pines is heard in our kettle. Let us dream of evanescence, and linger in the beautiful foolishness of things.

(Overleaf: *The iron kettle sighs like the wind in the pines.*)

THE SCHOOLS OF TEA

TEA IS A work of art and needs a master hand to bring out its noblest qualities. We have good and bad tea, as we have good and bad paintings —generally the latter. There is no single recipe for making the perfect tea, as there are no rules for producing a Titian or a Sesson. Each preparation of the leaves has its individuality, its special affinity with water and heat, its hereditary memories to recall, its own method of telling a story. The truly beautiful must be always in it. How much do we not suffer through the constant failure of society to recognise this simple and fundamental law of art and life; Lichihlai, a Sung poet, has sadly remarked that there were three most deplorable things in the world: the spoiling of fine youths through false education, the degradation of fine paintings through vulgar admiration, and the utter waste of fine tea through incompetent manipulation.

Like Art, Tea has its periods and its schools. Its evolution may be roughly divided into three main stages: the Boiled Tea, the Whipped Tea, and the Steeped Tea. We moderns belong to the last school. These several methods of appreciating the beverage are indicative of the spirit of the age in which they prevailed. For life is an expression, our unconscious actions the constant betrayal of our innermost thought. Confucius said that "man hideth not." Perhaps we reveal ourselves too much in small things because we have so little of the great to conceal. The tiny incidents of daily routine are as much a commentary of racial ideals as the highest flight of philosophy or poetry. Even as the difference in favourite vintage marks the separate idiosyncrasies of different periods and nationalities of Europe, so the Tea-ideals characterise the various moods of Oriental culture. The Cake-tea which was boiled, the Powdered-tea which was whipped, the Leaf-tea which was steeped, mark the distinct emotional impulses of the Tang, the Sung, and the Ming dynasties of China. If we were inclined to borrow the much-abused terminology of art classification, we might designate them respectively, the Classic, the Romantic, and the Naturalistic schools of Tea.

The tea-plant, a native of southern China, was known from very early times to Chinese botany and medicine. It is alluded to in the classics under the various names of Tou,

Tseh, Chung, Kha, and Ming, and was highly prized for possessing the virtues of relieving fatigue, delighting the soul, strengthening the will, and repairing the eye-sight. It was not only administered as an internal dose, but often applied externally in form of paste to alleviate rheumatic pains. The Taoists claimed it as an important ingredient of the elixir of immortality. The Buddhists used it extensively to prevent drowsiness during their long hours of meditation.

By the fourth and fifth centuries Tea became a favourite beverage among the inhabitants of the Yangtse Kiang valley. It was about this time that the modern ideograph Cha was coined, evidently a corruption of the classic Tou. The poets of the southern dynasties have left some fragments of their fervent adoration of the "froth of the liquid jade." Then emperors used to bestow some rare preparation of the leaves on their high ministers as a reward for eminent services. Yet the method of drinking tea at this stage was primitive in the extreme. The leaves were steamed, crushed in a mortar, made into a cake, and boiled together with rice, ginger, salt, orange peel, spices, milk, and sometimes with onions! The custom obtains at the present day among the Thibetans and various Mongolian tribes, who make a curious syrup of these ingredients. The use of lemon slices by the Russians, who learned to take tea from the Chinese caravansaries, points to the survival of the ancient method.

It needed the genius of the Tang dynasty to emancipate Tea from its crude state and lead to its final idealisation. With Luwuh in the middle of the eighth century we have our first apostle of tea. He was born in an age when Buddhism, Taoism, and Confucianism were seeking mutual synthesis. The pantheistic symbolism of the time was urging one to mirror the Universal in the Particular. Luwuh, a poet, saw in the Tea-service the same harmony and order which reigned through all things. In his celebrated work, the "Chaking" (The Holy Scripture of Tea) he formulated the Code of Tea. He has since been worshipped as the tutelary god of the Chinese tea merchants.

The "Chaking" consists of three volumes and ten chapters. In the first chapter Luwuh treats of the nature of the tea-plant, in the second of the implements for gathering the leaves, in the third of the selection of the leaves. According to him the best quality of the leaves must have "creases like the leathern boot of Tartar horsemen, curl like the dewlap of a mighty bullock, unfold like a mist rising out of a ravine, gleam like a lake touched by a zephyr, and be wet and soft like fine earth newly swept by rain."

The fourth chapter is devoted to the enumeration and description of the twenty-four members of the tea-equipage, beginning with the tripod brazier and ending with the bamboo cabinet for containing all these utensils. Here we notice Luwuh's predilection for Taoist symbolism. Also it is interesting to observe in this connection the influence of tea on Chinese ceramics. The Celestial porcelain, as is well known, had its origin in an attempt to reproduce the exquisite shade of jade, resulting, in the Tang dynasty, in the blue glaze of the south, and the white glaze of the north. Luwuh considered the blue as the ideal colour for the tea-cup, as it lent additional greenness to the beverage, whereas the white made it look pinkish and distasteful. It was because he used Cake-tea. Later on, when the teamasters of Sung took to the Powdered-tea, they preferred heavy bowls of blue-black and dark brown. The Mings, with their steeped tea, rejoiced in light ware of white porcelain.

In the fifth chapter Luwuh describes the method of making tea. He eliminates all ingredients except salt. He dwells also on the much-discussed question of the choice of water and the degree of boiling it. According to him, the mountain spring is the best, the river water and the spring water come next in the order of excellence. There are three stages of boiling: the first boil is when the little bubbles like the eye of fishes swim on the surface; the second boil is when the bubbles are like crystal beads rolling in a fountain; the third boil is when the billows surge wildly in the kettle. The Cake-tea is roasted before the fire until it becomes soft like a baby's arm and is shredded into powder betwen pieces of fine paper. Salt is put in the first boil, the tea in the second. At the third boil, a dipperful of cold water is poured into the kettle to settle the tea and revive the "youth of the water." Then the beverage was poured into cups and drunk. O nectar! The filmy leaflet hung like scaly clouds in a serene sky or floated like water-lilies on emerald streams. It was of such a beverage that Lotung, a Tang poet, wrote: "The first cup moistens my lips and throat, the second cup breaks my loneliness, the third cup searches my barren entrail but to find therein some five thousand volumes of odd ideographs. The fourth cup raises a slight perspiration—all the wrong of life passes away through my pores. At the fifth cup I am purified; the sixth cup calls me to the realms of immortals. The seventh cup—ah, but I could take no more! I only feel the breath of cool wind that rises in my sleeves. Where is Horaisan? Let me ride on this sweet breeze and waft away thither."

The remaining chapters of the "Chaking" treat of the vulgarity of the ordinary methods of tea-drinking, a historical summary of illustrious tea-drinkers, the famous tea-plantations of China, the possible variations of the tea-service, and illustrations of the tea-utensils. The last is unfortunately lost.

The appearance of the "Chaking" must have created considerable sensation at the time. Luwuh was befriended by the Emperor Taisung (763–779), and his fame attracted many followers. Some exquisites were said to have been able to detect the tea made by Luwuh from that of his disciples. One mandarin has his name immortalised by his failure to appreciate the tea of this great master.

In the Sung dynasty the whipped tea came into fashion

and created the second school of Tea. The leaves were ground to fine powder in a small stone mill, and the preparation was whipped in hot water by a delicate whisk made of split bamboo. The new process led to some change in the tea-equipage of Luwuh, as well as the choice of leaves. Salt was discarded forever. The enthusiasm of the Sung people for tea knew no bounds. Epicures vied with each other in discovering new varieties, and regular tournaments were held to decide their superiority. The Emperor Kiasung (1101–1124), who was too great an artist to be a well-behaved monarch, lavished his treasures on the attainment of rare species. He himself wrote a dissertation on the twenty kinds of tea, among which he prizes the "white tea" as of the rarest and finest quality.

The tea-ideal of the Sungs differed from the Tangs even as their notion of life differed. They sought to actualise what their predecessors tried to symbolise. To the Neo-Confucian mind the cosmic law was not reflected in the phenomenal world, but the phenomenal world was the cosmic law itself. Æons were but moments—Nirvana always within grasp. The Taoist conception that immortality lay in the eternal change permeated all their modes of thought. It was the process, not the deed, which was interesting. It was the completing, not the completion, which was really vital. Man came thus at once face to face with nature. A new meaning grew into the art of life. The tea began to be not a poetical pastime, but one of the methods of self-realisation. Wangyucheng eulogised tea as "flooding his soul like a direct appeal, that its delicate bitterness reminded him of the after-taste of a good counsel." Sotumpa wrote of the strength of the immaculate purity in tea which defied corruption as a truly virtuous man. Among the Buddhists, the southern Zen sect, which incorporated so much of Taoist doctrines, formulated an elaborate ritual of tea. The monks gathered before the image of Bodhi Dharma and drank tea out of a single bowl with the profound formality of a holy sacrament. It was this Zen ritual which finally developed into the Tea-ceremony of Japan in the fifteenth century.

Unfortunately the sudden outburst of the Mongol tribes in the thirteenth century, which resulted in the devastation and conquest of China under the barbaric rule of the Yuen Emperors, destroyed all the fruits of Sung culture. The native dynasty of the Mings which attempted re-nationalisation in the middle of the fifteenth century was harassed by internal troubles, and China again fell under the alien rule of the Manchus in the seventeenth century. Manners and customs changed to leave no vestige of the former times. The Powdered-tea is entirely forgotten. We find a Ming commentator at loss to recall the shape of the tea whisk mentioned in one of the Sung classics. Tea is now taken by steeping the leaves in hot water in a bowl or cup. The reason why the Western world is innocent of the older method of drinking tea is explained by the fact that Europe knew it only at the close of the Ming dynasty.

To the latter-day Chinese tea is a delicious beverage, but not an ideal. The long woes of his country have robbed him of the zest for the meaning of life. He has become modern, that is to say, old and disenchanted. He has lost that sublime faith in illusions which constitutes the eternal youth and vigour of the poets and ancients. He is an eclectic and politely accepts the traditions of the universe. He toys with Nature, but does not condescend to conquer or worship her. His Leaf-tea is often wonderful with its flower-like aroma, but the romance of the Tang and Sung ceremonials are not to be found in his cup.

Japan, which followed closely on the footsteps of Chinese civilisation, has known the tea in all its three stages. As early as the year 729 we read of the Emperor Shomu giving tea to one hundred monks at his palace in Nara. The leaves were probably imported by our ambassadors to the Tang Court and prepared in the way then in fashion. In 801 the monk Saicho brought back some seeds and planted them in Yeisan. Many tea-gardens are heard of in the succeeding centuries, as well as the delight of the aristocracy and priesthood in the beverage. The Sung tea reached us in 1191 with the return of Yeisaizenji, who went there to study the southern Zen school. The new seeds which he carried home were successfully planted in three places, one of which, the Uji district near Kioto, bears still the name of producing the best tea in the world. The southern Zen spread with marvellous rapidity, and with it the tea-ritual and the tea-ideal of the Sung. By the fifteenth century, under the patronage of the Shogun, Ashikaga Yoshimasa, the tea-ceremony is fully constituted and made into an independent and secular performance. Since then Teaism is fully established in Japan. The use of the steeped tea of the later China is comparatively recent among us, being only known since the middle of the seventeenth century. It has replaced the Powdered-tea in ordinary consumption, though the latter still continues to hold its place as the tea of teas.

It is in the Japanese tea ceremony that we see the culmination of tea-ideals. Our successful resistance of the Mongol invasion in 1281 had enabled us to carry on the Sung movement so disastrously cut off in China itself through the nomadic inroad. Tea with us became more than an idealisation of the form of drinking; it is a religion of the art of life. The beverage grew to be an excuse for the worship of purity and refinement, a sacred function at which the host and guest joined to produce for that occasion the utmost beatitude of the mundane. The tea-room was an oasis in the dreary waste of existence where weary travellers could meet to drink from the common spring of art appreciation. The ceremony was an improvised drama whose plot was woven about the tea, the flowers, and the paintings. Not a colour to disturb the tone of the room, not a sound to mar the rhythm of things, not a gesture to obtrude on the harmony, not a word to break the unity of the surroundings, all movements to be performed simply and naturally—such were the aims of the tea-ceremony. And strangely enough it was often successful. A subtle philosophy lay behind it all. Teaism was Taoism in disguise.

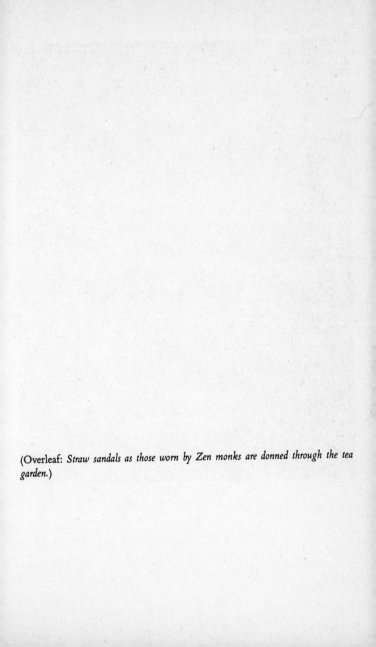

(Overleaf: *Straw sandals as those worn by Zen monks are donned through the tea garden.*)

TAOISM AND ZENNISM

THE CONNECTION of Zennism with tea is proverbial. We have already remarked that the tea-ceremony was a development of the Zen ritual. The name of Laotse, the founder of Taoism, is also intimately associated with the history of tea. It is written in the Chinese school manual concerning the origin of habits and customs that the ceremony of offering tea to a guest began with Kwanyin, a well-known disciple of Laotse, who first at the gate of the Han Pass presented to the "Old Philosopher" a cup of the golden elixir. We shall not stop to discuss the authenticity of such tales, which are valuable, however, as confirming the early use of the beverage by the Taoists. Our interest in Taoism and Zennism here lies mainly in those ideas regarding life and art which are so embodied in what we call Teaism.

It is to be regretted that as yet there appears to be no adequate presentation of the Taoist and Zen doctrines in any foreign language, though we have had several laudable attempts.

Translation is always a treason, and as a Ming author observes, can at its best be only the reverse side of a brocade—all the threads are there, but not the subtlety of colour or design. But, after all, what great doctrine is there which is easy to expound? The ancient sages never put their teachings in systematic form. They spoke in paradoxes, for they were afraid of uttering half-truths. They began by talking like fools and ended by making their hearers wise. Laotse himself, with his quaint humour, says, "If people of inferior intelligence hear of the Tao, they laugh immensely. It would not be the Tao unless they laughed at it."

The Tao literally means a Path. It has been severally translated as the Way, the Absolute, the Law, Nature, Supreme Reason, the Mode. These renderings are not incorrect, for the use of the term by the Taoists differs according to the subject-matter of the inquiry. Laotse himself spoke of it thus: "There is a thing which is all-containing, which was born before the existence of Heaven and Earth. How silent! How solitary! It stands alone and changes not. It revolves without danger to itself and is the mother of the universe. I do not know its name and so call it the Path. With reluctance I call it the Infinite. Infinity is the Fleeting, the Fleeting is the Vanishing, the Vanishing is the Reverting." The Tao is in the Passage rather than the Path. It is the spirit of Cosmic Change—the eternal growth which returns upon itself to produce new forms. It recoils upon itself like the dragon, the beloved symbol of the Taoists. It folds and unfolds as do the clouds. The Tao might be spoken of as the Great Transition. Subjectively it is the Mood of the Universe. Its Absolute is the Relative.

It should be remembered in the first place that Taoism, like its legitimate successor, Zennism, represents the individualistic trend of the Southern Chinese mind in contradistinction to the communism of Northern China which expressed itself in Confucianism. The Middle Kingdom is as vast as Europe and has a differentiation of idiosyncrasies marked by the two great river systems which traverse it. The Yangtse Kiang and Hoang Ho are respectively the Mediterranean and the Baltic. Even to-day, in spite of centuries of unification, the Southern Celestial differs in his thoughts and beliefs from his Northern brother as a member of the Latin race differs from the Teuton. In ancient days, when communication was even more difficult than at present, and especially during the feudal period, this difference in thought was most pronounced. The art and poetry of the one breathes an atmosphere entirely distinct from that of the other. In Laotse and his followers and in Kutsugen, the forerunner of the Yangtse Kiang nature-poets, we find an idealism quite inconsistent with the prosaic ethical notions of their contemporary northern writers. Laotse lived five centuries before the Christian Era.

The germ of Taoist speculation may be found long before the advent of Laotse, surnamed the Long-Eared. The archaic records of China, especially the Book of Changes, foreshadow his thought. But the great respect paid to the laws and customs of that classic period of Chinese civilisation which culminated with the establishment of the Chow dynasty in the twelfth century B.C., kept the development of individualism in check for a long while, so that it was not until after the disintegration of the Chow dynasty and the establishment of innumerable independent kingdoms that it was able to blossom forth in the luxuriance of free thought. Laotse and Soshi (Chuangtse) were both Southerners and the greatest exponents of the

New School. On the other hand Confucius with his numerous disciples aimed at retaining ancestral conventions. Taoism cannot be understood without some knowledge of Confucianism and vice versa.

We have said that the Taoist Absolute was the Relative. In ethics the Taoist railed at the laws and the moral codes of society, for to them right and wrong were but relative terms. Definition is always limitation—the "fixed" and "unchangeless" are but terms expressive of a stoppage of growth. Said Kutsugen, "The Sages move the world." Our standards of morality are begotten of the past needs of society, but is society to remain always the same? The observance of communal traditions involves a constant sacrifice of the individual to the state. Education, in order to keep up the mighty delusion, encourages a species of ignorance. People are not taught to be really virtuous, but to behave properly. We are wicked because we are frightfully self-conscious. We never forgive others because we know that we ourselves are in the wrong. We nurse a conscience because we are afraid to tell the truth to others; we take refuge in pride because we are afraid to tell the truth to ourselves. How can one be serious with the world when the world itself is so ridiculous! The spirit of barter is everywhere. Honour and Chastity! Behold the complacent salesman retailing the Good and True. One can even buy a so-called Religion, which is really but common morality sanctified with flowers and music. Rob the Church of her accessories and what remains behind? Yet the trusts thrive marvellously, for the prices are absurdly cheap—a prayer for a ticket to heaven, a diploma for an honourable citizenship. Hide yourself under a bushel quickly, for if your real usefulness were known to the world you would soon be knocked down to the highest bidder by the public auctioneer. Why do men and women like to advertise themselves so much? Is it not but an instinct derived from the days of slavery?

The virility of the idea lies not less in its power of breaking through contemporary thought than in its capacity for dominating subsequent movements. Taoism was an active power during the Shin dynasty, that epoch of Chinese unification from which we derive the name of China. It would be interesting had we time to note its influence on contemporary thinkers, the mathematicians, writers on law and war, the mystics and alchemists and the later nature-poets of the Yangtse Kiang. We should not even ignore those speculators on Reality who doubted whether a white horse was real because he was white, or because he was solid, nor the Conversationalists of the Six dynasties who like the Zen philosophers, revelled in discussions concerning the Pure and the Abstract. Above all we should pay homage to Taoism for what it has done toward the formation of the Celestial character, giving to it a certain capacity for reserve and refinement as "warm as jade." Chinese history is full of instances in which the votaries of Taoism, princes and hermits alike, followed with varied and interesting results the teachings of their creed. The tale will not be without its quota of instruction and amusement. It will be rich in anecdotes, allegories, and aphorisms. We would fain be on speaking terms with the delightful emperor who never died because he never lived. We may ride the wind with Liehtse and find it absolutely quiet because we ourselves are the wind, or dwell in mid-air with the Aged One of the Hoang Ho, who lived betwixt Heaven and Earth because he was subject to neither the one nor the other. Even in that grotesque apology for Taoism which we find in China at the present day, we can revel in a wealth of imagery impossible to find in any other cult.

But the chief contribution of Taoism to Asiatic life has been in the realm of aesthetics. Chinese historians have always spoken of Taoism as the "art of being in the world," for it deals with the present—ourselves. It is in us that God meets with Nature, and yesterday parts from tomorrow. The Present is the moving Infinity, the legitimate sphere of the Relative. Relativity seeks Adjustment; Adjustment is Art. The art of life lies in a constant readjustment to our surroundings. Taoism accepts the mundane as it is and, unlike the Confucians and the Buddhists, tries to find beauty in our world of woe and worry. The Sung allegory of the Three Vinegar Tasters explains admirably the trend of the three doctrines. Sakyamuni, Confucius, and Laotse once stood before a jar of vinegar—the emblem of life— and each dipped in his fingers to taste the brew. The matter-of-fact Confucius found it sour, the Buddha called it bitter, and Laotse pronounced it sweet.

The Taoists claimed that the comedy of life could be made more interesting if everyone would preserve the unities. To keep the proportion of things and give place to others without losing one's own position was the secret of success in the mundane drama. We must know the whole play in order to properly act our parts; the conception of totality must never be lost in that of the individual. This Laotse illustrates by his favourite metaphor of the Vacuum. He claimed that only in vacuum lay the truly essential. The reality of a room, for instance, was to be found in the vacant space enclosed by the roof and walls, not in the roof and walls themselves. The usefulness of a water pitcher dwelt in the emptiness where water might be put, not in the form of the pitcher or the material of which it was made. Vacuum is all potent because all containing. In vacuum alone motion becomes possible. One who could make of himself a vacuum into which others might freely enter would become master of all situations. The whole can always dominate the part.

These Taoists' ideas have greatly influenced all our theories of action, even to those of fencing and wrestling. Jiu-jitsu, the Japanese art of self-defence, owes its name to a passage in the Taoteiking. In jiu-jitsu one seeks to draw out and exhaust the enemy's strength by non-resistance, vacuum, while conserving one's own strength for victory in the final struggle. In art the importance of the same principle is illustrated by the value of suggestion. In leaving something unsaid the beholder is given a chance to complete the idea and thus a great masterpiece irresistibly rivets your attention until you seem to become actually a part of it. A vacuum is there for you to enter and fill up to the full measure of your aesthetic emotion.

He who had made himself master of the art of living was the Real Man of the Taoist. At birth he enters the realm of dreams only to awaken to reality at death. He tempers his own brightness in order to merge himself into the obscurity of others. He is "reluctant, as one who crosses a stream in winter; hesitating, as one who fears the neighbourhood; respectful, like a guest; trembling, like ice that is about to melt; unassuming, like a piece of wood not yet carved; vacant, like a valley; formless, like troubled waters." To him the three jewels of life were Pity, Economy, and Modesty.

If now we turn our attention to Zennism we shall find that it emphasises the teachings of Taoism. Zen is a name derived from the Sanscrit word Dhyana, which signifies meditation. It claims that through consecrated meditation may be attained supreme self-realisation. Meditation is one of the six ways through which Buddhahood may be reached, and the Zen sectarians affirm that Sakyamuni laid special stress on this method in his later teachings, handing down the rules to his chief disciple Kashiapa. According to their tradition Kashiapa, the first Zen patriarch, imparted the secret to Ananda, who in turn passed it on to successive patriarchs until it reached Bodhi Dharma, the twenty-eighth. Bodhi Dharma came to Northern China in the early half of the sixth century and was the first patriarch of Chinese Zen. There is much uncertainty about the history of these patriarchs and their doctrines. In its philosophical aspect early Zennism seems to have affinity on one hand to the Indian Negativism of Nagarjuna and on the other to the Gnan philosophy formulated by Sancharacharya. The first teaching of Zen as we know it at the present day must be attributed to the sixth Chinese patriarch Yeno (637–713), founder of Southern Zen, so-called from the fact of its predominance in Southern China. He is closely followed by the great Baso (died 788), who made of Zen a living influence in Celestial life. Hiakujo (719–814), the pupil of Baso, first instituted the Zen monastery and established a ritual and regulations for its government. In the discussions of the Zen school after the time of Baso we find the play of the Yangtse-Kiang mind causing an accession of native modes of thought in contrast to the former Indian idealism. Whatever sectarian pride may assert to the contrary, one cannot help being impressed by the similarity of Southern Zen to the teachings of Laotse, and the Taoist Conversationalists. In the Taoteiking we already find allusions to the importance of self-concentration and the need of properly regulating the breath—essential points in the practice of Zen meditation. Some of the best commentaries on the Book of Laotse have been written by Zen scholars.

Zennism, like Taoism, is the worship of Relativity. One master defines Zen as the art of feeling the polar star in the southern sky. Truth can be reached only through the comprehension of opposites. Again, Zennism, like Taoism, is a strong advocate of individualism. Nothing is real except that which concerns the working of our own minds. Yeno, the sixth patriarch, once saw two monks watching the flag of a pagoda fluttering in the wind. One said, "It is the wind that moves," the other said, "It is the flag that moves"; but Yeno explained to them that the real movement was neither of the wind nor the flag, but of something within their own minds. Hiakujo was walking in the forest with a disciple when a hare scurried off at their approach. "Why does the hare fly from you?" asked Hiakujo. "Because he is afraid of me," was the answer. "No," said the master, "it is because you have a murderous instinct." This dialogue recalls that of Soshi (Chuangtse), the Taoist. One day Soshi was walking on the bank of a river with a friend. "How delightfully the fishes are enjoying themselves in the water!" exclaimed Soshi. His friend spake to him thus: "You are not a fish; how do you know that the fishes are enjoying themselves!" "You are not myself," returned Soshi; "how do you know that I do not know that the fishes are enjoying themselves?"

Zen was often opposed to the precepts of orthodox Buddhism even as Taoism was opposed to Confucianism. To the transcendental insight of the Zen, words were but an incumbrance to thought; the whole sway of Buddhist scriptures only commentaries on personal speculation. The followers of Zen aimed at direct communion with the inner nature of things, regarding their outward accessories only as impediments to a clear perception of Truth. It was this love of the Abstract that led the Zen to prefer black and white sketches to the elaborately coloured paintings of the classic Buddhist School. Some of the Zen even became iconoclastic as a result of their endeavour to recognise the Buddha in themselves rather than through images and symbolism. We find Tankawosho breaking up a wooden statue of Buddha on a wintry day to make a fire. "What sacrilege!" said the horror-stricken bystander. "I wish to get the Shali out of the ashes," calmly rejoined the Zen. "But you certainly will not get Shali from this image!" was the angry retort, to which Tanka replied, "If I do not, this is certainly not a Buddha and I am committing no sacrilege." Then he turned to warm himself over the kindling fire.

A special contribution of Zen to Eastern thought was its recognition of the mundane as of equal importance with the spiritual. It held that in the great relation of things there was no distinction of small and great, an atom possessing equal possibilities with the universe. The seeker for perfection must discover in his own life the reflection of the inner light. The organisation of the Zen monastery was very significant of this point of view. To every member, except the abbot, was assigned some special work in the caretaking of the monastery, and curiously enough, to the novices were committed the lighter duties, while to the most respected and advanced monks were given the more irksome and menial tasks. Such services formed a part of the Zen discipline and every least action must be done absolutely perfectly. Thus many a weighty discussion ensued while weeding the garden, paring a turnip, or serving tea. The whole ideal of Teaism is a result of this Zen conception of greatness in the smallest incidents of life. Taoism furnished the basis for aesthetic ideals, Zennism made them practical.

(Overleaf: *The subdued lighting and simple interior relax the mind, yet sharpen the senses.*)

THE TEA-ROOM

To EUROPEAN architects brought up on the traditions of stone and brick construction, our Japanese method of building with wood and bamboo seems scarcely worthy to be ranked as architecture. It is but quite recently that a competent student of Western architecture has recognised and paid tribute to the remarkable perfection of our great temples. Such being the case as regards our classic architecture, we could hardly expect the outsider to appreciate the subtle beauty of the tea-room, its principles of construction and decoration being entirely different from those of the West.

The tea-room (the Sukiya) does not pretend to be other than a mere cottage—a straw hut, as we call it. The original ideographs for Sukiya mean the Abode of Fancy. Latterly the various tea-masters substituted various Chinese characters according to their conception of the tea-room, and the term Sukiya may signify the Abode of Vacancy or the Abode of the Unsymmetrical. It is an Abode of Fancy inasmuch as it is an ephemeral structure built to house a poetic impulse. It is an Abode of Vacancy inasmuch as it is devoid of ornamentation except for what may be placed in it to satisfy some aesthetic need of the moment. It is an Abode of the Unsymmetrical inasmuch as it is consecrated to the worship of Imperfect, purposely leaving some thing unfinished for the play of the imagination to complete. The ideals of Teaism have since the sixteenth century influenced our architecture to such a degree that the ordinary Japanese interior of the present day, on account of the extreme simplicity and chasteness of its scheme of decoration, appears to foreigners almost barren.

The first independent tea-room was the creation of Sen no Soyeki, commonly known by his later name of Rikiu, the greatest of all tea-masters, who, in the sixteenth century, under the patronage of Taiko Hideyoshi, instituted and brought to a high state of perfection the formalities of the Tea-ceremony. The proportions of the tea-room had been previously determined by Joō—a famous tea-master of the fifteenth century. The early tea-room consisted merely of a portion of the ordinary drawing-room partitioned off by screens for the purpose of the tea-gathering. The portion partitioned off was called the Kakoi (enclosure), a name still applied to those tea-rooms which are built into a house and are not independent constructions. The Sukiya consists of the tea-room proper, designed to accommodate not more than five persons, a number suggestive of the saying "more than the Graces and less than the Muses," an anteroom (midsuya) where the tea utensils are washed and arranged before being brought in, a portico (machiai) in which the guests wait until they receive the summons to enter the tea-room, and a garden path (the roji) which connects the machiai with the tea-room. The tea-room is unimpressive in appearance. It is smaller than the smallest of Japanese houses, while the materials used in its construction are intended to give the suggestion of refined poverty. Yet we must remember that all this is the result of profound artistic forethought, and that the details have been worked out with care perhaps even greater than that expended on the building of the richest palaces and temples. A good tea-room is more costly than an ordinary mansion, for the selection of its materials, as well as its workmanship, requires immense care and precision. Indeed the carpenters employed by the tea-masters form a distinct and highly honoured class among artisans, their work being no less delicate than that of the makers of lacquer cabinets.

The tea-room is not only different from any production of Western architecture, but also contrasts strongly with the classical architecture of Japan itself. Our ancient noble edifices, whether secular or ecclesiastical, were not to be despised even as regards their mere size. The few that have been spared in the disastrous conflagrations of centuries are still capable of aweing us by the grandeur and richness of their decoration. Huge pillars of wood from two to three feet in diameter and from thirty to forty feet high, supported, by a complicated network of brackets, the enormous beams which groaned under the weight of the tile-covered slanting roofs. The material and mode of construction, though weak against fire, proved itself strong against earthquakes, and was well suited to the climatic conditions of the country. In the Golden Hall of Horiu-ji and the Pagoda of Yakushiji, we have noteworthy examples of the durability of our wooden architecture. These buildings have practically stood intact for nearly twelve centuries. The interior of the old temples and palaces was profusely decorated. In the Hoōdo temple at

Uji, dating from the tenth century, we can still see the elaborate canopy and gilded baldachinos, many-coloured and inlaid with mirrors and mother-of-pearl, as well as remains of the paintings and sculpture which formerly covered the walls. Later, at Nikko and in the Nijo castle in Kioto, we see structural beauty sacrificed to a wealth of ornamentation which in colour and exquisite detail equals the utmost gorgeousness of Arabian or Moorish effort.

The simplicity and purism of the tea-room resulted from emulation of the Zen monastery. A Zen monastery differs from those of other Buddhist sects inasmuch as it is meant only to be a dwelling place for the monks. Its chapel is not a place of worship or pilgrimage, but a college room where the students congregate for discussion and the practise of meditation. The room is bare except for a central alcove in which, behind the altar, is a statue of Bodhi Dharma, the founder of the sect, or of Sakyamuni attended by Kashiapa and Ananda, the two earliest Zen patriarchs. On the altar, flowers and incense are offered up in memory of the great contributions which these sages made to Zen. We have already said that it was the ritual instituted by the Zen monks of successively drinking tea out of a bowl before the image of Bodhi Dharma, which laid the foundations of the tea-ceremony. We might add here that the altar of the Zen chapel was the prototype of the Tokonoma—the place of honour in a Japanese room where paintings and flowers are placed for the edification of the guests.

All our great tea-masters were students of Zen and attempted to introduce the spirit of Zennism into the actualities of life. Thus the room, like the other equipments of the tea-ceremony, reflects many of the Zen doctrines. The size of the orthodox tea-room, which is four mats and a half, or ten feet square, is determined by a passage in the Sutra of Vikramadytia. In that interesting work, Vikramadytia welcomes the Saint Manjushiri and eighty-four thousand disciples of Buddha in a room of this size—an allegory based on the theory of the non-existence of space to the truly enlightened. Again the roji, the garden path which leads from the machiai to the tea-room, signified the first stage of meditation—the passage into self-illumination. The roji was intended to break connection with the outside world, and to produce a fresh sensation conducive to the full enjoyment of aestheticism in the tea-room itself. One who has trodden this garden path cannot fail to remember how his spirit, as he walked in the twilight of evergreens over the regular irregularities of the stepping-stones, beneath which lay dried pine needles, and passed beside the moss-covered granite lanterns, became uplifted above ordinary thoughts. One may be in the midst of a city, and yet feel as if he were in the forest far away from the dust and din of civilisation. Great was the ingenuity displayed by the tea-masters in producing these effects of serenity and purity. The nature of the sensations to be aroused in passing through the roji differed with different tea-masters. Some, like Rikiu, aimed at utter loneliness, and claimed the secret of making a roji was contained in the ancient ditty:

I looked beyond;
Flowers are not,
Nor tinted leaves.
On the sea beach
A solitary cottage stands
In the waning light
Of an autumn eve.

Others, like Kobori Enshiu, sought for a different effect. Enshiu said the idea of the garden path was to be found in the following verses:

A cluster of summer trees,
A bit of the sea,
A pale evening moon.

It is not difficult to gather his meaning. He wished to create the attitude of a newly awakened soul still lingering amid shadowy dreams of the past, yet bathing in the sweet unconsciousness of a mellow spiritual light, and yearning for the freedom that lay in the expanse beyond.

Thus prepared the guest will silently approach the sanctuary, and, if a samurai, will leave his sword on the rack beneath the eaves, the tea-room being pre-eminently the house of peace. Then he will bend low and creep into the room through a small door not more than three feet in height. This proceeding was incumbent on all guests—high and low alike—and was intended to inculcate humility. The order of precedence having been mutually agreed upon while resting in the machiai, the guests one by one will enter noiselessly and take their seats, first making obeisance to the picture or flower arrangement on the Tokonoma. The host will not enter the room until all the guests have seated themselves and quiet reigns with nothing to break the silence save the note of the boiling water in the iron kettle. The kettle signs well, for pieces of iron are so arranged in the bottom as to produce a peculiar melody in which one may hear the echoes of a cataract muffled by clouds, of a distant sea breaking among the rocks, a rainstorm sweeping through a bamboo forest, or of the soughing of pines on some faraway hill.

Even in the daytime the light in the room is subdued, for the low eaves of the slanting roof admit but few of the sun's rays. Everything is sober in tint from the ceiling to the floor; the guests themselves have carefully chosen garments of unobtrusive colours. The mellowness of age is over all, everything suggestive of recent acquirement being tabooed save only the one note of contrast furnished by the bamboo dipper and the linen napkin, both immaculately white and new. However faded the tea-room and the tea-equipage may seem, everything is absolutely clean. Not a particle of dust will be found in the darkest corner, for if any exists the host is not a tea-master. One of the first requisites of a tea-master is the knowledge of how to sweep, clean, and wash, for there is an art in cleaning and dusting. A piece of antique metal work must not be attacked with the unscrupulous zeal of the Dutch house-wife. Dripping water from a flower vase need not be wiped away, for it may be suggestive of dew and coolness.

In this connection there is a story of Rikiu which well illustrates the ideas of cleanliness entertained by the tea-masters. Rikiu was watching his son Shoan as he swept and watered the garden path. "Not clean enough," said Rikiu, when Shoan had finished his task, and bade him try again. After a weary hour the son turned to Rikiu: "Father, there is nothing more to be done. The steps have been washed for the third time, the stone lanterns and the trees are well sprinkled with water, moss and lichens are shining with a fresh verdure; not a twig, not a leaf have I left on the ground." "Young fool," chided the tea-master, "that is not the way a garden path should be swept." Saying this, Rikiu stepped into the garden, shook a tree and scattered over the garden gold and crimson leaves, scraps of the brocade of autumn! What Rikiu demanded was not cleanliness alone, but the beautiful and the natural also.

The name, Abode of Fancy, implies a structure created to meet some individual artistic requirement. The tea-room is made for the tea-master, not the tea-master for the tea-room. It is not intended for posterity and is therefore ephemeral. The idea that everyone should have a house of his own is based on an ancient custom of the Japanese race, Shinto superstition ordaining that every dwelling should be evacuated on the death of its chief occupant. Perhaps there may have been some unrealised sanitary reason for this practice. Another early custom was that a newly built house should be provided for each couple that married. It is on account of such customs that we find the Imperial capitals so frequently removed from one site to another in ancient days. The rebuilding, every twenty years, of Ise Temple, the supreme shrine of the Sun Goddess, is an example of one of these ancient rites which still obtain at the present day. The observance of these customs was only possible with some such form of construction as that furnished by our system of wooden architecture, easily pulled down, easily built up. A more lasting style, employing brick and stone, would have rendered migrations impracticable, as indeed they became when the more stable and massive wooden construction of China was adopted by us after the Nara period.

With the predominance of Zen individualism in the fifteenth century, however, the old idea became imbued with a deeper significance as conceived in connection with the tea-room. Zennism, with the Buddhist theory of evanescence and its demands for the mastery of spirit over matter, recognised the house only as a temporary refuge for the body. The body itself was but as a hut in the wilderness, a flimsy shelter made by tying together the grasses that grew around—when these ceased to be bound together they again became resolved into the original waste. In the tea-room fugitiveness is suggested in the thatched roof, frailty in the slender pillars, lightness in the bamboo support, apparent carelessness in the use of commonplace materials. The eternal is to be found only in the spirit which, embodied in these simple surroundings, beautifies them with the subtle light of its refinement.

That the tea-room should be built to suit some individual taste is an enforcement of the principle of vitality in art. Art, to be fully appreciated, must be true to contemporaneous life. It is not that we should ignore the claims of posterity, but that we should seek to enjoy the present more. It is not that we should disregard the creations of the past, but that we should try to assimilate them into our consciousness. Slavish conformity to traditions and formulas fetters the expression of individuality in architecture. We can but weep over those senseless imitations of European buildings which one beholds in modern Japan. We marvel why, among the most progressive Western nations, architecture should be so devoid of originality, so replete with repetitions of obsolete styles. Perhaps we are now passing through an age of democratisation in art, while awaiting the rise of some princely master who shall establish a new dynasty. Would that we loved the ancients more and copied them less! It has been said that the Greeks were great because they never drew from the antique.

The term, Abode of Vacancy, besides conveying the Taoist theory of the all-containing, involves the conception of a continued need of change in decorative motives. The tea-room is absolutely empty, except for what may be placed there temporarily to satisfy some aesthetic mood. Some special art object is brought in for the occasion, and everything else is selected and arranged to enhance the beauty of the principal theme. One cannot listen to different pieces of music at the same time, a real comprehension of the beautiful being possible only through concentration upon some central motive. Thus it will be seen that the system of decoration in our tea-rooms is opposed to that which obtains in the West, where the interior of a house is often converted into a museum. To a Japanese, accustomed to simplicity of ornamentation and frequent change of decorative method, a Western interior permanently filled with a vast array of pictures, statuary, and bric-à-brac gives the impression of mere vulgar display of riches. It calls for a mighty wealth of appreciation to enjoy the constant sight of even a masterpiece, and limitless indeed must be the capacity for artistic feeling in those who can exist day after day in the midst of such confusion of colour and form as is to be often seen in the homes of Europe and America.

The Abode of the Unsymmetrical suggests another phase of our decorative scheme. The absence of symmetry in Japanese art objects has been often commented on by Western critics. This, also, is a result of a working out through Zennism of Taoist ideals. Confucianism, with its deep-seated idea of dualism, and Northern Buddhism with its worship of a trinity, were in no way opposed to the expression of symmetry. As a matter of fact, if we study the ancient bronzes of China or the religious arts of the Tang dynasty and the Nara period, we shall recognise a constant striving after symmetry. The decoration of our classical interiors was decidedly regular in its arrangement. The Taoist and Zen conception of perfection, however, was different. The dynamic nature of their philosophy laid more stress upon the process through which perfection was sought than upon perfection itself. True beauty could be discovered only by one who mentally completed the incomplete. The virility of life and art lay in its possibilities for growth. In the tea-room it is left for each guest in imagination to complete the total effect in relation to himself. Since Zennism has become the prevailing mode of thought, the art of the extreme Orient has purposely avoided the symmetrical as expressing not only completion, but repetition. Uniformity of design was considered as fatal to the freshness of imagination. Thus, landscapes, birds, and flowers became the favourite subjects for depiction rather than the human figure, the latter being present in the person of the beholder himself. We are often too much in evidence as it is, and in spite of our vanity even self-regard is apt to become monotonous.

In the tea-room the fear of repetition is a constant presence. The various objects for the decoration of a room should be so selected that no colour or design shall be repeated. If you have a living flower, a painting of flowers is not allowable. If you are using a round kettle, the water pitcher should be angular. A cup with a black glaze should not be associated with a tea-caddy of black lacquer. In placing a vase or an incense burner on the tokonoma, care should be taken not to put it in the exact centre, lest it divide the space into equal halves. The pillar of the tokonoma should be of a different kind of wood from the other pillars, in order to break any suggestion of monotony in the room.

Here again the Japanese method of interior decoration differs from that of the Occident, where we see objects arrayed symmetrically on mantelpieces and elsewhere. In Western houses we are often confronted with what appears to us useless reiteration. We find it trying to talk to a man while his full-length portrait stares at us from behind his back. We wonder which is real, he of the picture or he who talks, and feel a curious conviction that one of them must be fraud. Many a time have we sat at a festive board contemplating, with a secret shock to our digestion, the representation of abundance on the dining-room walls. Why these pictured victims of chase and sport, the elaborate carvings of fishes and fruit? Why the display of family plates, reminding us of those who have dined and are dead?

The simplicity of the tea-room and its freedom from vulgarity make it truly a sanctuary from the vexations of the outer world. There and there alone can one consecrate himself to undisturbed adoration of the beautiful. In the sixteenth century the tea-room afforded a welcome respite from labour to the fierce warriors and statesmen engaged in the unification and reconstruction of Japan. In the seventeenth century, after the strict formalism of the Tokugawa rule had been developed, it offered the only opportunity possible for the free communion of artistic spirits. Before a great work of art there was no distinction between daimyo, samurai, and commoner. Nowadays industrialism is making true refinement more and more difficult all the world over. Do we not need the tea-room more than ever?

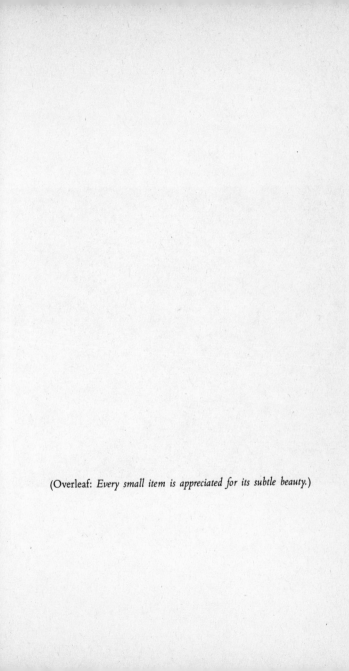

(Overleaf: *Every small item is appreciated for its subtle beauty.*)

ART APPRECIATION

HAVE YOU HEARD the Taoist tale of the Taming of the Harp?

Once in the hoary ages in the Ravine of Lungmen stood a Kiri tree, a veritable king of the forest. It reared its head to talk to the stars; its roots struck deep into the earth, mingling their bronzed coils with those of the silver dragon that slept beneath. And it came to pass that a mighty wizard made of this tree a wondrous harp, whose stubborn spirit should be tamed but by the greatest of musicians. For long the instrument was treasured by the Emperor of China, but all in vain were the efforts of those who in turn tried to draw melody from its strings. In response to their utmost strivings there came from the harp but harsh notes of disdain, ill-according with the songs they fain would sing. The harp refused to recognise a master.

At last came Peiwoh, the prince of harpists. With tender hand he caressed the harp as one might seek to soothe an unruly horse, and softly touched the chords. He sang of nature and the seasons, of high mountains and flowing waters, and all the memories of the tree awoke! Once more the sweet breath of spring played amidst its branches. The young cataracts, as they danced down the ravine, laughed to the budding flowers. Anon were heard the dreamy voices of summer with its myriad insects, the gentle pattering of rain, the wail of the cuckoo. Hark! a tiger roars—the valley answers again. It is autumn; in the desert night, sharp like a sword gleams the moon upon the frosted grass. Now winter reigns, and through the snow-filled air swirl flocks of swans and rattling hailstones beat upon the boughs with fierce delight.

Then Peiwoh changed the key and sang of love. The forest swayed like an ardent swain deep lost in thought. On high, like a haughty maiden, sewpt a cloud bright and fair; but passing, trailed long shadows on the ground, black like despair. Again the mode was changed; Peiwoh sang of war, of clashing steel and trampling steeds. And in the harp arose the tempest of Lungmen, the dragon rode the lightning, the thundering avalanche crashed through the hills. In ecstacy the Celestial monarch asked Peiwoh wherein lay the secret of his victory. "Sire," he replied, "others have failed because they sang but of themselves. I left the harp to choose its theme, and knew not truly whether the harp had been Peiwoh or Peiwoh were the harp."

This story well illustrates the mystery of art appreciation. The masterpiece is a symphony played upon our finest feelings. True art is Peiwoh, and we the harp of Lungmen. At the magic touch of the beautiful the secret chords of our being are awakened, we vibrate and thrill in response to its call. Mind speaks to mind. We listen to the unspoken, we gaze upon the unseen. The master calls forth notes we know not of. Memories long forgotten all come back to us with a new significance. Hopes stifled by fear, yearnings that we dare not recognise, stand forth in new glory. Our mind is the canvas on which the artists lay their colour; their pigments are our emotions; their chiaroscuro the light of joy, the shadow of sadness. The masterpiece is of ourselves, as we are of the masterpiece.

The sympathetic communion of minds necessary for art appreciation must be based on mutual concession. The spectator must cultivate the proper attitude for receiving the message, as the artist must know to impart it. The tea-master, Kobori Enshiu, himself a daimyo, has left to us these memorable words: "Approach a great painting as thou wouldst approach a great prince." In order to understand a masterpiece, you must lay yourself low before it and await with bated breath its least utterance. An eminent Sung critic once made a charming confession. Said he: "In my young days I praised the master whose pictures I liked, but as my judgment matured I praised myself for liking what the masters had chosen to have me like." It is to be deplored that so few of us really take pains to study the moods of the masters. In our stubborn ignorance we refuse to render them this simple courtesy, and thus often miss the rich repast of beauty spread before our very eyes. A master has always something to offer, while we go hungry solely because of our own lack of appreciation.

To the sympathetic a masterpiece becomes a living reality towards which we feel drawn in bonds of comradeship. The masters are immortal, for their loves and fears live in us over and over again. It is rather the soul than the hand, the man than the technique, which appeals to us—the more human the call the deeper is our response. It is because of this secret understanding between the master and ourselves that in poetry or romance we suffer and rejoice with the hero and heroine. Chikamatsu, our Japanese Shakespeare, has laid down as one of the first principles of dramatic composition the importance of taking the audience into the confidence of the author. Several of his pupils submitted plays for his approval, but only one of the pieces appealed to him. It was a play somewhat resembling the Comedy of Errors, in which twin brethren suffer through mistaken identity. "This," said Chikamatsu, "has the proper spirit of the drama, for it takes the audience into consideration. The public is permitted to know more than the actors. It knows where the mistake lies, and pities the poor figures on the board who innocently rush to their fate."

The great masters both of the East and the West never forgot the value of suggestion as a means for taking the spectator into their confidence. Who can contemplate a masterpiece without being awed by the immense vista of thought presented to our consideration? How familiar and sympathetic are they all; how cold in contrast the modern commonplaces! In the former we feel the warm outpouring of a man's heart; in the latter only a formal salute. Engrossed in his technique, the modern rarely rises above himself. Like the musicians who vainly invoked the Lungmen harp, he sings only of himself. His works may be nearer science, but are further from humanity. We have an old saying in Japan that a woman cannot love a man who is truly vain, for there is no crevice in his heart for love to enter and fill up. In art vanity is equally fatal to sympathetic feeling, whether on the part of the artist or the public.

Nothing is more hallowing than the union of kindred spirits in art. At the moment of meeting, the art lover transcends himself. At once he is and is not. He catches a glimpse of Infinity, but words cannot voice his delight, for the eye has no tongue. Freed from the fetters of matter, his spirit moves in the rhythm of things. It is thus that art becomes akin to religion and ennobles mankind. It is this which makes a masterpiece something sacred. In the old days the veneration in which the Japanese held the work of the great artist was intense. The tea-masters guarded their treasures with religious secrecy, and it was often necessary to open a whole series of boxes, one within another, before reaching the shrine itself—the silken wrapping within whose soft folds lay the holy of holies. Rarely was the object exposed to view, and then only to the initiated.

At the time when Teaism was in the ascendency the Taiko's generals would be better satisfied with the present of a rare work of art than a large grant of territory as a reward of victory. Many of our favourite dramas are based on the loss and recovery of a noted masterpiece. For instance, in one play the palace of Lord Hosokawa, in which was preserved the celebrated painting of Daruma by Sesson, suddenly takes fire through the negligence of the samurai in charge. Resolved at all hazards to rescue the precious painting, he rushes into the burning building and seizes the kakemono, only to find all means of exit cut off by the flames. Thinking only of the picture, he slashes open his body with his sword, wraps his torn sleeve about the Sesson, and plunges it into the gaping wound. The fire is at last extinguished. Among the smoking embers is found a half-consumed corpse, within which reposes the treasure uninjured by the fire. Horrible as such tales are, they illustrate the great value that we set upon a masterpiece, as well as the devotion of a trusted samurai.

We must remember, however, that art is of value only to the extent that it speaks to us. It might be a universal language if we ourselves were universal in our sympathies.

Our finite nature, the power of tradition and convention-ality, as well as our hereditary instincts, restrict the scope of our capacity for artistic enjoyment. Our very individuality establishes in one sense a limit to our understanding; and our aesthetic personality seeks its own affinities in the creations of the past. It is true that with cultivation our sense of art appreciation broadens, and we become able to enjoy many hitherto unrecognised expressions of beauty. But, after all, we see only our own image in the universe—our particular idiosyncrasies dictate the mode of our per-ceptions. The tea-masters collected only objects which fell strictly within the measure of their individual apprecia-tion.

One is reminded in this connection of a story concern-ing Kobori Enshiu. Enshiu was complimented by his dis-ciples on the admirable taste he had displayed in the choice of his collection. Said they, "Each piece is such that no one could help admiring. It shows that you had better taste than had Rikiu, for his collection could only be appreciated by one beholder in a thousand." Sorrowfully Enshiu replied: "This only proves how commonplace I am. The great Rikiu dared to love only those objects which personally appealed to him, whereas I unconsciously cater to the taste of the majority. Verily, Rikiu was one in a thousand among tea-masters."

It is much to be regretted that so much of the apparent enthusiasm for art at the present day has no foundation in real feeling. In this democratic age of ours men clamour for what is popularly considered the best, regardless of their feelings. They want the costly, not the refined; the fashionable, not the beautiful. To the masses, contemplation of illustrated periodicals, the worthy product of their own industrialism, would give more digestible food for artistic enjoyment than the early Italians or the Ashikaga masters, whom they pretend to admire. The name of the artist is more important to them than the quality of the work. As a Chinese critic complained many centuries ago, "People criticise a picture by their ear." It is this lack of genuine appreciation that is responsible for the pseudo-classic horrors that to-day greet us wherever we turn.

Another common mistake is that of confusing art with archaeology. The veneration born of antiquity is one of the best traits in the human character, and fain would we have it cultivated to a greater extent. The old masters are rightly to be honoured for opening the path to future enlightenment. The mere fact that they have passed unscathed through centuries of criticism and come down to us still covered with glory commands our respect. But we should be foolish indeed if we valued their achievement simply on the score of age. Yet we allow our historical sympathy to override our aesthetic discrimination. We offer flowers of approbation when the artist is safely laid in his grave. The nineteenth century, pregnant with the theory of evolution, has moreover created in us the habit of losing sight of the individual in the species. A collector is anxious to acquire specimens to illustrate a period or a school, and forgets that a single masterpiece can teach us more than any number of the mediocre products of a given period or school. We classify too much and enjoy too little. The sacrifice of the aesthetic to the so-called scientific method of exhibition has been the bane of many museums.

The claims of contemporary art cannot be ignored in any vital scheme of life. The art of to-day is that which really belongs to us: it is our own reflection. In condemning it we but condemn ourselves. We say that the present age possesses no art—who is responsible for this? It is indeed a shame that despite all our rhapsodies about the ancients we pay so little attention to our own possibilities. Struggling artists, weary souls lingering in the shadow of cold disdain! In our self-centred century, what inspiration do we offer them? The past may well look with pity at the poverty of our civilisation; the future will laugh at the barrenness of our art. We are destroying art in destroying the beautiful in life. Would that some great wizard might from the stem of society shape a mighty harp whose strings would resound to the touch of genius.

(Overleaf: *Delicate flowers, picked at dawn, represent nature.*)

FLOWERS

IN THE TREMBLING grey of a spring dawn, when the birds were whispering in mysterious cadence among the trees, have you not felt that they were talking to their mates about the flowers? Surely with mankind the appreciation of flowers must have been coeval with the poetry of love. Where better than in a flower, sweet in its unconsciousness, fragrant because of its silence, can we image the unfolding of a virgin soul? The primeval man in offering the first garland to his maiden thereby transcended the brute. He became human in thus rising above the crude necessities of nature. He entered the realm of art when he perceived the subtle use of the useless.

In joy or sadness, flowers are our constant friends. We eat, drink, sing, dance, and flirt with them. We wed and christen with flowers. We dare not die without them. We have worshipped with the lily, we have meditated with the lotus, we have charged in battle array with the rose and the chrysanthemum. We have even attempted to speak in the language of flowers. How could we live without them? It frightens one to conceive of a world bereft of their presence. What solace do they not bring to the bedside of the sick, what a light of bliss to the darkness of weary spirits? Their serene tenderness restores to us our waning confidence in the universe even as the intent gaze of a beautiful child recalls our lost hopes. When we are laid low in the dust it is they who linger in sorrow over our graves.

Sad as it is, we cannot conceal the fact that in spite of our companionship with flowers we have not risen very far above the brute. Scratch the sheepskin and the wolf within us will soon show his teeth. It has been said that man at ten is an animal, at twenty a lunatic, at thirty a failure, at forty a fraud, and at fifty a criminal. Perhaps he becomes a criminal because he has never ceased to be an animal. Nothing is real to us but hunger, nothing sacred except our own desires. Shrine after shrine has crumbled before our eyes; but one altar forever is preserved, that whereon we burn incense to the supreme idol—ourselves. Our god is great, and money is his Prophet! We devastate nature in order to make sacrifice to him. We boast that we have conquered Matter and forget that it is Matter that has enslaved us.

What atrocities do we not perpetrate in the name of culture and refinement!

Tell me, gentle flowers, teardrops of the stars, standing in the garden, nodding your heads to the bees as they sing of the dews and the sunbeams, are you aware of the fearful doom that awaits you? Dream on, sway and frolic while you may in the gentle breezes of summer. To-morrow a ruthless hand will close around your throats. You will be wrenched, torn asunder limb by limb, and borne away from your quiet homes. The wretch, she may be passing fair. She may say how lovely you are while her fingers are still moist with your blood. Tell me, will this be kindness? It may be your fate to be imprisoned in the hair of one whom you know to be heartless or to be thrust into the buttonhole of one who would not dare to look you in the face were you a man. It may even be your lot to be confined in some narrow vessel with only stagnant water to quench the maddening thirst that warns of ebbing life.

Flowers, if you were in the land of the Mikado, you might some time meet a dread personage armed with scissors and a tiny saw. He would call himself a Master of Flowers. He would claim the rights of a doctor and you would instinctively hate him, for you know a doctor always seeks to prolong the troubles of his victims. He would cut, bend, and twist you into those impossible positions which he thinks it proper that you should assume. He would contort your muscles and dislocate your bones like any osteopath. He would burn you with red-hot coals to stop your bleeding, and thrust wires into you to assist your circulation. He would diet you with salt, vinegar, alum, and sometimes, vitriol. Boiling water would be poured on your feet when you seemed ready to faint. It would be his boast that he could keep life within you for two or more weeks longer than would have been possible without his treatment. Would you not have preferred to have been killed at once when you were first captured? What were the crimes you must have committed during your past incarnation to warrant such punishment as this?

The wanton waste of flowers among Western communities is even more appalling than the way they are treated by Eastern Flower-Masters. The number of flowers cut daily to adorn the ballrooms and banquet-tables of Europe and America, to be thrown away on the morrow, must be something enormous; if strung together they might garland a continent. Beside this utter carelessness of life, the guilt of the Flower-Master becomes insignificant. He, at least, respects the economy of nature, selects his victims with careful foresight, and after death does honour to their remains. In the West the display of flowers seems to be a part of the pageantry of wealth—the fancy of a moment. Whither do they all go, these flowers, when the revelry is over? Nothing is more pitiful than to see a faded flower remorselessly flung upon a dung heap.

Why were the flowers born so beautiful and yet so hapless? Insects can sting, and even the meekest of beasts will fight when brought to bay. The bird whose plumage is sought to deck some bonnet can fly from its pursuer, the furred animal whose coat you covet for your own may hide at your approach. Alas! The only flower known to have wings is the butterfly; all others stand helpless before the destroyer. If they shriek in their death agony their cry never reaches our hardened ears. We are ever brutal to those who love and serve us in silence, but the time may come when, for our cruelty, we shall be deserted by these best friends of ours. Have you not noticed that the wild flowers are becoming scarcer every year? It may be that their wise men have told them to depart till man becomes more human. Perhaps they have migrated to heaven.

Much may be said in favour of him who cultivates plants. The man of the pot is far more humane than he of the scissors. We watch with delight his concern about water and sunshine, his feuds with parasites, his horror of frosts, his anxiety when the buds come slowly, his rapture when the leaves attain their lustre. In the East the art of floriculture is a very ancient one, and the loves of a poet and his favourite plant have often been recorded in story and song. With the development of ceramics during the Tang and Sung dynasties we hear of wonderful receptacles made to hold plants, not pots, but jewelled palaces. A special attendant was detailed to wait upon each flower and to wash its leaves with soft brushes made of rabbit hair. It has been written that the peony should be bathed by a handsome maiden in full costume, that a winter-plum should be watered by a pale, slender monk. In Japan, one of the most popular of the No dances, the Hachinoki, composed during the Ashikaga period, is based upon the story of an impoverished knight, who, on a freezing night, in lack of fuel for a fire, cuts his cherished plants in order to entertain a wandering friar. The friar is in reality no other than Hojo Tokiyori, the Haroun-Al-Raschid of our tales, and the sacrifice is not without its reward. This opera never fails to draw tears from a Tokio audience even to-day.

Great precautions were taken for the preservation of delicate blossoms. Emperor Huensung, of the Tang dynasty, hung tiny golden bells on the branches in his garden to keep off the birds. He it was who went off in the springtime with his court musicians to gladden the flowers with soft music. A quaint tablet, which tradition ascribes to Yoshitsune, the hero of our Arthurian legends, is still extant in one of the Japanese monasteries. It is a notice put up for the protection of a certain wonderful plum-tree, and appeals to us with the grim humour of a warlike age. After referring to the beauty of the blossoms, the inscription says: "Whoever cuts a single branch of this tree shall forfeit a finger therefor." Would that such laws could be enforced nowadays against those who wantonly destroy flowers and mutilate objects of art!

Yet even in the case of pot flowers we are inclined to suspect the selfishness of man. Why take the plants from their homes and ask them to bloom mid strange surroundings? Is it not like asking the birds to sing and mate cooped up in cages? Who knows but that the orchids feel stifled by the artificial heat in your conservatories and hopelessly long for a glimpse of their own Southern skies?

The ideal lover of flowers is he who visits them in their native haunts, like Taoyuenming, who sat before a broken bamboo fence in converse with the wild chrysanthemum, or Linwosing, losing himself amid mysterious fragrance as he wandered in the twilight among the plum-blossoms of the Western Lake. 'Tis said that Chowmushih slept in a boat so that his dreams might mingle with those of the lotus. It was this same spirit which moved the Empress Komio, one of our most renowned Nara sovereigns, as she sang: "If I pluck thee, my hand will defile thee, O Flower! Standing in the meadows as thou art, I offer thee to the Buddhas of the past, of the present, of the future."

However, let us not be too sentimental. Let us be less luxurious but more magnificent. Said Laotse: "Heaven and earth are pitiless." Said Kobodaishi: "Flow, flow, flow, flow, the current of life is ever onward. Die, die, die, die, death comes to all." Destruction faces us wherever we turn. Destruction below and above, destruction behind and before. Change is the only Eternal—why not as welcome Death as Life? They are but counterparts one of the other—the Night and Day of Brahma. Through the disintegration of the old, re-creation becomes possible. We have worshipped Death, the relentless goddess of mercy, under many different names. It was the shadow of the All-devouring that the Gheburs greeted in the fire. It is the icy purism of the sword-soul before which Shinto-Japan prostrates herself even to-day. The mystic fire consumes our weakness, the sacred sword cleaves the bondage of desire. From our ashes springs the phoenix of celestial hope, out of the freedom comes a higher realisation of manhood.

Why not destroy flowers if thereby we can evolve new forms ennobling the world idea? We only ask them to join in our sacrifice to the beautiful. We shall atone for the deed by consecrating ourselves to Purity and Simplicity. Thus reasoned the tea-masters when they established the Cult of Flowers.

Anyone acquainted with the ways of our tea- and flower-masters must have noticed the religious veneration with which they regard flowers. They do not cull at random, but carefully select each branch or spray with an eye to the artstic composition they have in mind. They would be ashamed should they chance to cut more than were absolutely necessary. It may be remarked in this connection that they always associate the leaves, if there be any, with the flower, for their object is to present the whole beauty of plant life. In this respect, as in many others, their method differs from that pursued in Western countries. Here we are apt to see only the flower stems, heads, as it were, without body, stuck promiscuously into a vase.

When a tea-master has arranged a flower to his satisfaction he will place it on the Tokonoma, the place of honour in a Japanese room. Nothing else will be placed near it which might interfere with its effect, not even a painting, unless there be some special aesthetic reason for the combination. It rests there like an enthroned prince, and the guests or disciples on entering the room will salute it with a profound bow before making their addresses to the host. Drawings from masterpieces are made and published for the edification of amateurs. The amount of literature on the subject is quite voluminous. When the flower fades, the master tenderly consigns it to the river or carefully buries it in the ground. Monuments even are sometimes erected to their memory.

The birth of the Art of Flower Arrangement seems to be simultaneous with that of Teaism in the fifteenth century. Our legends ascribe the first flower arrangement to those early Buddhist saints who gathered the flowers strewn by the storm and, in their infinite solicitude for all living things, placed them in vessels of water. It is said that Soami, the great painter and connoisseur of the court of Ashikaga Yoshimasa, was one of the earliest adepts at it. Juko, the tea-master, was one of his pupils, as was also Senno, the founder of the house of Ikenobo, a family as illustrious in the annals of flowers as was that of the Kanos in painting. With the perfecting of the tea-ritual under Rikiu, in the latter part of the sixteenth century, flower arrangement also attains its full growth. Rikiu and his successors, the celebrated Oda Wuraku, Furuta Oribe, Koyetsu, Kobori Enshiu, Katagiri Sekishiu, vied with each other in forming new combinations. We must remember, however, that the flower worship of the tea-masters formed only a part of their aesthetic ritual, and was not a distinct religion by itself. A flower arrangement, like the other works of art in the tea-room, was subordinated to the total scheme of decoration. Thus Sekishiu ordained that white plum-blossoms should not be made use of when snow lay in the garden. "Noisy" flowers were relentlessly banished from the tea-room. A flower arrangement by a tea-master loses its significance if removed from the place for which it was originally intended, for its lines and proportions have been specially worked out with a view to its surroundings.

The adoration of the flower for its own sake begins with the rise of "Flower-Masters," toward the middle of the seventeenth century. It now becomes independent of the tea-room and knows no law save that the vase imposes on it. New conceptions and methods of execution now become possible, and many were the principles and schools resulting therefrom. A writer in the middle of the last century said he could count over one hundred different schools of flower arrangement. Broadly speaking, these divide themselves into two main branches, the Formalistic and the Naturalesque. The Formalistic schools, led by the Ikenobos, aimed at a classic idealism corresponding to that of the Kano-academicians. We possess records of arrangements by the early masters of this school which almost reproduce the flower paintings of Sansetsu and Tsunenobu. The Naturalesque school, on the other hand, as its name implies, accepted nature as its model, only imposing such modifications of form as conduced to the expression of artistic unity. Thus we recognise in its works the same impulses which formed the Ukiyoe and Shijo schools of painting.

It would be interesting, had we time, to enter more fully than is now possible into the laws of composition and detail formulated by the various flower-masters of this period, showing, as they would, the fundamental theories which governed Tokugawa decoration. We find them referring to the Leading Principle (Heaven), the Subordinate Principle (Earth), the Reconciling Principle (Man), and any flower arrangement which did not embody these principles was considered barren and dead. They also dwelt much on the importance of treating a flower in its three different aspects, the Formal, the Semi-Formal, and the Informal. The first might be said to represent flowers in the stately costume of the ballroom, the second in the easy elegance of afternoon dress, the third in the charming deshabille of the boudoir.

Our personal sympathies are with the flower arrangements of the tea-master rather than with those of the flower-master. The former is art in its proper setting and appeals to us on account of its true intimacy with life. We should like to call this school the Natural in contradistinction to the Naturalesque and Formalistic schools. The tea-master deems his duty ended with the selection of the flowers, and leaves them to tell their own story. Entering a tea-room in late winter, you may see a slender spray of wild cherries in combination with a budding camellia; it is an echo of departing winter coupled with the prophecy of spring. Again, if you go into a noon-tea on some irritatingly hot summer day, you may discover in the darkened coolness of the Tokonoma a single lily in a hanging vase; dripping with dew, it seems to smile at the foolishness of life.

A solo of flowers is interesting, but in a concerto with painting and sculpture the combination becomes entrancing. Sekishiu once placed some water-plants in a flat receptacle to suggest the vegetation of lakes and marshes, and on the wall above he hung a painting by Soami of wild ducks flying in the air. Shoha, another tea-master, combined a poem on the Beauty of Solitude by the Sea with a bronze incense burner in the form of a fisherman's hut and some wild flowers of the beach. One of the guests has recorded that he felt in the whole composition the breath of waning autumn.

Flower stories are endless. We shall recount but one more. In the sixteenth century the morning-glory was as yet a rare plant with us. Rikiu had an entire garden planted with it, which he cultivated with assiduous care. The fame of his convolvuli reached the ear of the Taiko, and he expressed a desire to see them, in consequence of which Rikiu invited him to a morning tea at his house. On the appointed day the Taiko walked through the garden, but nowhere could he see any vestige of the convolvulus. The ground had been leveled and strewn with fine pebbles and sand. With sullen anger the despot entered the tea-room, but a sight waited him there which completely restored his humour. On the Tokonoma, in a rare bronze of Sung workmanship, lay a single morning-glory—the queen of the whole garden!

In such instances we see the full significance of the

Flower Sacrifice. Perhaps the flowers appreciated the full significance of it. They are not cowards, like men. Some flowers glory in death—certainly the Japanese cherry blossoms do, as they freely surrender themselves to the winds. Anyone who has stood before the fragrant avalanche at Yoshino or Arashiyama must have realised this. For a moment they hover like bejewelled clouds and dance above the crystal streams; then, as they sail away on the laughing waters, they seem to say: "Farewell, O Spring! We are on to Eternity."

(Overleaf: *The whisk is deftly raised from the bowl. . . . The tea is ready.*)

TEA-MASTERS

In RELIGION the Future is behind us. In art the Present is the eternal. The tea-master held that real appreciation of art is only possible to those who make of it a living influence. Thus they sought to regulate their daily life by the high standard of refinement which obtained in the tea-room. In all circumstances serenity of mind should be maintained, and conversation should be so conducted as never to mar the harmony of the surroundings. The cut and colour of the dress, the poise of the body, and the manner of walking could all be made expressions of artistic personality. These were matters not to be lightly ignored, for until one has made himself beautiful he has no right to approach beauty. Thus the tea-master strove to be something more than the artist— art itself. It was the Zen of aestheticism. Perfection is everywhere if we only choose to recognise it. Rikiu loved to quote an old poem which says: "To those who long only for flowers, fain would I show the full-blown spring which abides in the toiling buds of snow-covered hills."

Manifold indeed have been the contributions of the tea-masters to art. They completely revolutionised the classical architecture and interior decorations, and established the new style which we have described in the chapter of the tea-room, a style to whose influence even the palaces and monasteries built after the sixteenth century have all been subject. The many-sided Kobori Enshiu has left notable examples of his genius in the Imperial villa of Katsura, the castles of Nagoya and Nijo, and the monastery of Kohoan. All the celebrated gardens of Japan were laid out by the tea-masters. Our pottery would probably never have attained its high quality of excellence if the tea-masters had not lent to it their inspiration, the manufacture of the utensils used in the tea-ceremony calling forth the utmost expenditure of ingenuity on the part of our ceramists. The Seven Kilns of Enshiu are well known to all students of Japanese pottery. Many of our textile fabrics bear the names of tea-masters who conceived their colour or design. It is impossible, indeed, to find any department of art in which the tea-masters have not left marks of their genius. In painting and lacquer it seems almost superfluous to mention the immense service they have rendered. One of the greatest schools of painting owes its origin to the tea-master Honnami-Koyetsu, famed also as a lacquer artist and potter. Beside his works, the splendid creation of his grandson, Koho, and of his grandnephews, Korin and Kenzan, almost fall into the shade. The whole Korin school, as it is generally designated, is an expression of Teaism. In the broad lines of this school we seem to find the vitality of nature herself.

Great as has been the influence of the tea-masters in the field of art, it is as nothing compared to that which they have exerted on the conduct of life. Not only in the usages of polite society, but also in the arrangement of all our domestic details, do we feel the presence of the tea-masters. Many of our delicate dishes, as well as our way of serving food, are their inventions. They have taught us to dress only in garments of sober colours. They have instructed us in the proper spirit in which to approach flowers. They have given emphasis to our natural love of simplicity, and shown us the beauty of humility. In fact, through their teachings tea has entered the life of the people.

Those of us who know not the secret of properly regulating our own existence on this tumultuous sea of foolish troubles which we call life are constantly in a state of misery while vainly trying to appear happy and contented. We stagger in the attempt to keep our moral equilibrium, and see forerunners of the tempest in every cloud that floats on the horizon. Yet there is joy and beauty in the roll of the billows as they sweep outward toward eternity. Why not enter into their spirit, or, like Liehtse, ride upon the hurricane itself?

He only who has lived with the beautiful can die beautifully. The last moments of the great tea-masters were as full of exquisite refinement as had been their lives. Seeking always to be in harmony with the great rhythm of the universe, they were ever prepared to enter the unknown. The "Last Tea of Rikiu" will stand forth forever as the acme of tragic grandeur.

Long had been the friendship between Rikiu and the Taiko Hideyoshi, and high the estimation in which the great warrior held the tea-master. But the friendship of a despot is ever a dangerous honour. It was an age rife with treachery, and men trusted not even their nearest kin. Rikiu was no servile courtier, and had often dared to differ in argument with his fierce patron. Taking advantage of the coldness which had for some time existed between the Taiko and Rikiu, the enemies of the latter accused him of being implicated in a conspiracy to poison the despot. It was whispered to Hideyoshi that the fatal potion was to be administered to him with a cup of the green beverage prepared by the tea-master. With Hideyoshi suspicion was sufficient ground for instant execution, and there was no appeal from the will of the angry ruler. One privilege alone was granted to the condemned—the honour of dying by his own hand.

On the day destined for his self-immolation, Rikiu invited his chief disciples to a last tea-ceremony. Mournfully at the appointed time the guests met at the portico. As they look into the garden path the trees seem to shudder, and in the rustling of their leaves are heard the whispers of homeless ghosts. Like solemn sentinels before the gates of Hades stand the grey stone lanterns. A wave of rare incense is wafted from the tea-room; it is the summons which bids the guests to enter. One by one they advance and take their places. In the Tokonoma hangs a kakemono—a wonderful writing by an ancient monk dealing with the evanescence of all earthly things. The singing kettle, as it boils over the brazier, sounds like some cicada pouring forth his woes to departing summer. Soon the host enters the room. Each in turn is served with tea, and each in turn silently drains his cup, the host last of all. According to established etiquette, the chief guest now asks permission to examine the tea-equipage. Rikiu places the various articles before them with the kakemono. After all have expressed admiration of their beauty, Rikiu presents one of them to each of the assembled company as a souvenir. The bowl alone he keeps. "Never again shall this cup, polluted by the lips of misfortune, be used by man." He speaks, and breaks the vessel into fragments.

The ceremony is over; the guests with difficulty restraining their tears, take their last farewell and leave the room. One only, the nearest and dearest, is requested to remain and witness the end. Rikiu then removes his tea-gown and carefully folds it upon the mat, thereby disclosing the immaculate white death robe which it had hitherto concealed. Tenderly he gazes on the shining blade of the fatal dagger, and in exquisite verse thus addresses it:

Welcome to thee,
O sword of eternity!
Through Buddha
And through Daruma alike
Thou hast cleft thy way.

  With a smile upon his face Rikiu passed forth into the unknown.

AFTERWORD

CHANOYU has always existed at the core of my life, but if it had not been for Kakuzo Okakura's *The Book of Tea*, the scope of my life's work might have been quite different. When I think back, one event from among the confused memories of the war period remains especially vivid. I was being trained with a special attack unit of the naval air force. Before their mission my comrades wanted to share a bowl of tea, and so with the compact set of utensils I had with me, I performed the preparation of tea. Sitting cross-legged in their uniforms, the men drank, one by one, from the bowls placed before them. Many of them set out the next day never to return, but in my mind remained the composure of that last tea gathering—the equanimity of friends amid the seeming hush of a photograph.

With the war's end, we were all looking about for new directions and new values to guide us into the future. Returning to my home one day, I happened upon the scene of my father, the grand tea master, making tea for a group of the occupying American forces. I entered the tea room with conflicting emotions. These soldiers had been our enemies a few months before; yet my father was now calmly serving them tea. This memory has stayed with me these many years, and it was fundamental to my resolution to spread this spirit of chanoyu around the world and to make it my life's work. At a time when Japan was emerging from the shadow of war and the ashes of destruction covered the land, chanoyu represented progress and light.

Okakura wrote *The Book of Tea* in 1906, as Japan was facing an influx of Western ideas and institutions, in danger of losing its cultural bearings. The postwar period found Japan in a similar situation: the fall of the old system and the call for a new, democratic form of government. Under the guidance of the Occupation forces, the new constitution—based upon Western models—was adopted. The ideas were so alien that a new language had to be devised to express them. My memory of this time includes a lecture given by a military officer at Waseda University. His point was that the Japanese people should not merely adopt the democratic institutions of the West, but also look to the democratic ideals formulated in their own heritage, in the traditions of chanoyu, as set forth in *The Book of Tea*.

Although Okakura originally wrote *The Book of Tea* to introduce Asian thought and civilization to the West, its unique perspective—standing within the traditions of Asian culture but expressed in the light of Western modes of thought—provided affirmation of the central values of Japanese life.

During my first trips to the United states in the 1950s, I was to discover how widespread was the influence of Okakura's work. Chanoyu was virtually unknown in many of the places I visited, and items basic for its practice, such as *tatami*, were not to be found. But as my wife and I improvised mats for our demonstration of chanoyu, spreading sheets and securing them with black tape to suggest the borders of *tatami*, we found that, in a sense, our way had already been prepared. People who knew nothing else of chanoyu, who knew little about any aspect of Japanese life, had read Okakura's book.

To select tea as a symbol for Asian life was Okakura's genius. And it was certainly a daring stroke, for it juxtaposed the leaves of an ordinary-looking bush—even if Okakura referred to it as the "queen of camellias"—with the industrial and technological might of the West. "Tea" represented the world of nature as traditionally viewed in the East, as well as the daily life of common people. It united a diversity of people across the Asian continent and reminded us of the close bonds interwoven in our cultures over the centuries.

This "tea" developed as a way of life—a path of practice in search of spiritual fulfillment. This "tea" was chanoyu. Based on the notion that we can never attain inner peace without a deliberate effort to free ourselves from the cares and desires of the world, chanoyu offered us the chance to step beyond daily attachments and to delve to the roots of our human being. In doing so, chanoyu embraced a universal concern.

As a path of practice, chanoyu offers a comprehensive model for life. It serves as a constant reminder of the basic values—arising from the age-old wisdom and experience of the traditions of Asia—of a people over time. It preaches no religious doctrine. Its great strength lies in the concreteness of its forms and its foundation in the most fundamental of human activities: sitting together with others, partaking of a meal, and drinking tea. Sen Rikyu (1522–1591), the man who established the foundations of chanoyu as we know it today, said: "Chanoyu is just a matter of gathering wood, boiling water, and drinking tea; nothing else is involved."

As an expression of the principles underlying the way of chanoyu, Rikyu used the phrase "harmony, respect, purity tranquillity" (*wa, kei, sei, jaku*). In chanoyu, practitioners enter a world in which—through the common consent, discipline, and long training of all the participants—these human ideals prevail, in contrast to the busyness of everyday activity.

The phrase "harmony, respect, purity, tranquillity" occurs in the Zen literature of China, and is not an original Japanese formulation. It consciously looks to the great paths of spiritual cultivation, and surely today as in Rikyu's day, we can appreciate these ideals as being valuable to all human beings.

Harmony and reverence suggest virtues of social interaction, while purity and tranquillity have a stronger personal meaning. However, they are all closely intertwined, the one implying the others, indeed assuming the others. Thus, all have concrete implications for the practitioner's relationship with the other participants and the environment of tea itself as well as for the interior condition of each individual.

Harmony

Harmony strongly suggests a Confucian virtue—the atmosphere of accord. The reason chanoyu insists upon careful manners in all aspects of interaction is, perhaps most of all, to achieve this state. Many people who observe chanoyu for the first time find the adherence to formal demeanor rigid and confining, but the informality often favored by the young is not necessarily liberating.

Rules of social life have been instituted precisely to free us from the erratic impulses of selfishness and anger, and to enable us to relate to others at a level that transcends immediate conditions, thoughts, feelings. Rituals are perhaps less appreciated today than at any other time in human history, but in chanoyu they do allow us to create for ourselves havens of solemnity and inner solitude—a time and circumstance to honor what we know to be most important in our lives. Manners in chanoyu—though they prescribe precisely when and even how deeply to bow, when to speak and what topics are appropriate for conversation—impart to us the ability to discipline our inner lives, and to train ourselves to encounter any situation with self-composure.

The emphasis on harmony in chanoyu gave rise to one of chanoyu's most distinctive features: the practice of social equality within the tea room. This does not mean that all social distinctions are simply swept away, or that order is left to chance. On the contrary, the order of the guests is carefully determined beforehand, and the roles and places of the main guest and succeeding guests are set. By adhering to such rules, however, we are freed to come together at a human level, leaving behind outside entanglements and joining together in the world of chanoyu.

This spirit is expressed in the unique entrance to the tea room. Rikyu, in transforming the four-and-a-half *tatami* mat room into a thatched tea hut, created a very small entrance called a *nijiriguchi*, literally a "crawling-in entrance." This architectural device reveals the essence of chanoyu.

People who were involved in chanoyu in Rikyu's time were mainly feudal lords, upper-class warriors, and rich merchants. All guests at a tea gathering who were of the warrior class had first to remove their swords—the symbols of their rank—before crawling through this entrance. Even the ruler of the nation was required to do this. By thus entering the tea room, all assumed an equal posture, having cast off their status in the strict feudal social structure and having passed into a realm in which people are respected, above all, for their humanity.

Among the buildings the Urasenke compound, there is a tea room known as Kan'untei, built by the third generation tea master, Sen Sotan (1578–1658). It is one of the oldest of the Urasenke tea rooms, and its appearance and mood is characteristic of the seventeenth century. One of the distinguishing features of this room is its ceiling, which is divided into three sections of different levels and construction: formal (*shin*), semi-formal (*gyo*), and informal (*so*). The Empress Tofukumon'in, the wife of Emperor Gomizuno'o, was a student of Sotan's. At the palace, she would sit, as was customary for a person of her rank, in an elevated area of the room. When she came to Sotan's house, where there was no such area, she sat on the same level as any other student. Out of personal respect for her, however, Sotan provided her a place beneath the formal level of the ceiling. Here was both a regard for ordinary manners and an expression, in chanoyu, of seeing beyond the accidents of circumstance.

"The true aristocrat is the one who is free of anxiety"

(*buji kore kinin*), said the Zen master Rinzai (d. 866). Practitioners of chanoyu cherish these words, for to be "free of anxiety" (*buji*—literally, "nothing to do" or "safe") is an ideal aspired to. Thus occurs the irony that although in the mundane world it is the aristocrats and captains of society who rule, in the tea room it is those who have achieved their own interior solitude who hold the place of eminence. In these ways, harmony implies a strong democratic spirit.

This principle of harmony is related not only to the social dimension of a tea gathering, but also to the conduct of our lives in accord with nature. While contemporary life offers us access to many conveniences that allow us to carry on daily life without regard for the natural world, at the heart of chanoyu lies an intricate and subtle interaction with one's environment. This is especially apparent in the awareness of seasonal changes that is so much a part of chanoyu, from the choice of utensils and foods, to the method of preparing the tea.

When Rikyu was asked to explain the secrets of using the brazier and the hearth—that is, the essential distinctions in preparing tea during the winter and the summer—he replied:

In summer, impart a sense of deep coolness; in winter, a feeling of warmth. Lay the charcoal so that it heats the water; prepare the tea so that it is pleasing. These are all the secrets.

The question asked of Rikyu was based on the assumption that there was some hidden transmission of tea manner known only to advanced students, but Rikyu responded by stating the fundamental attitude of a host. It was a simple matter. The questioner, taken aback, complained, "That is something everyone knows." "If so," Rikyu rejoined, "try preforming as I have said. I will be your guest, and perhaps become your student."

Such ideals may of course be shared by many, even as we may lack only the time to fulfill them. The practice of chanoyu, however, is the deliberate refusal to postpone one's essential existence as a human being, in the full awareness of how exacting, and yet how important, that task can be. It is to live with a refined attention to detail—the flowers of the season, the sound of water poured onto stone, the time at which evening turns to dusk—not because these things will enlarge the self, but because they bring our lives into harmony with that which transcends the self.

In chanoyu, the methods of laying the charcoal have been passed down through generations of tea masters. The precise number of pieces of charcoal, and even their sizes and shapes, are prescribed, as are the order in which they are arranged and their exact position on the bed of sifted ash. Yet our study of these methods is carried on for a lifetime, for the intent is not to achieve a perfect imitation of those time-honored methods, but to lay the charcoal unfailingly "so that it heats the water"—so that it lights quickly, burns evenly, and heats the kettle of water at the proper time with no waste. The beauty and economy of the burning charcoal, which retains the shape of a round branch cut crosswise, its bark still intact, is also the beauty and economy of the moving hand of the master, which bespeaks a deeper harmony with the moment of the tea gathering.

Rikyu, in his response noted above, consciously alluded to a story familiar to the masters of art in Japan. A Chinese Zen master named Dorin, renouncing the mundane life, took to living in a tree. The poet Po Chu-i went to see what he could learn from him.

Po said, "Master! Your dwelling is precarious." The Zen

master answered, "It is your way of life—which involves yourself in the world and which neglects its real nature—that is precarious."

Po asked, "What is the Buddha's teaching?"

Dorin said, "Avoid wrong acts and perform good."

"Any child of three knows that," replied the poet.

The monk said, "A child of three may know, but even an old man of eighty will go astray in the practice."

In this story is contained the fundamental attitude of tea practitioners, both past and present. A lifetime of training may bring knowledge in a complex of traditions and fields—ceramics and textiles, incense, lacquerware, cooking, the writings of Zen masters, and the classics of Japanese poetry, to name a few—yet it is always what is most basic that is most difficult. The papered windows and *tatami* floors of the tea room do not of themselves create a haven apart from the hard responsibility of life; but for the practitioner, they do bring man nearer to an inner reality, freeing us all of our futile flight from a discordant precariousness.

As regards another rule of chanoyu, Rikyu said: "Arrange the flowers as they are in the field." Okakura, in his chapter "Flowers," discusses various types of flower arrangement, noting his preference for *chabana*, the kind of arrangement that derives from Rikyu's principle. Again, Rikyu's rule may be simple, but its mastery requires years of practice. Like other aspects of chanoyu, the arranging of *chabana* is a lifelong discipline.

People sometimes wonder at the paradox—the careful arrangement made to evoke naturalness. Merely to reproduce a scene of flowers in the field is not the aim. The naturalness that is the result can only come from understanding, then capturing the essence of the flowers themselves. Moreover, in the still space of the tea room, the flowers adorning the alcove, removed from the entanglements of temporal life, possess an immediacy not apparent when viewed in nature. Indeed, they exist solely in the present and impress upon us the particularity of their individual existence, just as they are. As Okakura notes:

> They are not cowards, like men. Some flowers glory in death—certainly the Japanese cherry blossoms do, as they freely surrender themselves to the winds.... As they sail away on the laughing waters, they seem to say: "Farewell, O Spring! We are on to Eternity."

Crucial to the appreciation of flowers in chanoyu is a profound awareness that transcends any human-centered view of the world.

Respect

On a personal level, the principle of harmony implies a spirit of reverence and humility. There can be no genuine acknowledgment of others unless one is able to discard the self-attachments that dominate life in society. Indeed, the failure to perceive the deepest humanity of others is one of the greatest causes of strife in the world.

The need for a spirit of reverence and respect is apparent in various aspects of chanoyu. Okakura discusses this in his brilliant chapter, "Art Appreciation," where he relates the parable of the harp. Only in the hands of someone who submits to the latent song within it will the harp give forth music. So it is, says Okakura, for those who stand before works of art.

Much of chanoyu involves training one to see the world around us. Okakura even speaks of chanoyu as a "religion of aestheticism." To see, in chanoyu, is to let the distorting lens of social custom and valuation fall away, and to perceive and appreciate things for themselves. It is important to realize that many of the items treasured in chanoyu were not created as "art," but were discovered and adopted from among the most ordinary of household utensils.

Hence, the objects valued in chanoyu are not judged against an ideal of formal beauty. To borrow a cliché, beauty lies in the eye of the beholder, and in chanoyu, this eye is nurtured through the spirit of respect.

The significance of respect in chanoyu is expressed well in a story about Sotan. One day a close friend of Sotan's, a priest at Daitokuji, sent a young acolyte to deliver a particularly fine sprig of white camellia blossoms to him. On the way, however, the main blossom fell off its stem. After weighing his alternatives, the boy decided to deliver the fallen blossom and to apologize for his carelessness. The respect inherent in the acolyte's sentiment is exemplary; it shows a reverence for quite ordinary objects. But even more noteworthy is Sotan's reaction, which was to place the stem in a vase and hang it on the alcove pillar and to lay the fallen blossom on the floor of the alcove. In this manner, out of his respect for his friend's thoughtfulness, the boy's efforts, and the flower itself, the camellia took on new life within the realm of chanoyu.

In the scope of human relationships, the principle

of respect means to have no designs on others, to be free of the calculation to impress or compete. Rikyu taught:

> It is good for the spirits of guest and host to be in mutual accord. But to want to be in accord is harmful. If both guest and host have attained a grasp of the way, a sense of harmony will arise spontaneously.

Genuine harmony cannot be attained through the self-conscious endeavor of the participants, but must arise free of their intentions. That is, it comes about only when it is based on mutual respect and on a selflessness achieved through long discipline and practice.

One of the most revealing expressions of the quality of respect in chanoyu is the phrase, "this meeting—but once in a lifetime" (*ichigo ichie*). These words define the attitude of the practitioner during a tea gathering, and are derived from the instruction of Jo'o, Rikyu's teacher:

> From the moment you enter the garden pathway until the time you depart, you should hold the host in most respectful esteem, in the spirit that the gathering will occur but once in your life.

This attitude of cherishing each moment is nurtured through training in chanoyu, and has value to all human encounters. When the tea student receives instruction from a teacher—or when we meet our associates, our friends, our family—this sense of the significance of the present is the manifestation of sincerity. In chanoyu, sincerity extends as well to one's relationship with the environment. The bowl in our hands comes to exist as more than the name of a kiln, more than some formal concept, when it is held for the "one and only time," when the pressures of our own self-centered lives are forgotten at the moment of drinking from it.

Purity

It is often said that the aspect of purity is the most characteristically Japanese element of chanoyu—an element in accord with the religious spirit of Shinto. Certainly the emphasis on purity in chanoyu is apparent everywhere. The tea room is always carefully cleaned and prepared before a gathering, and it is further purified with incense after the guests have entered. Similarly, the walkways are carefully sprinkled with water shortly before the arrival of guests. Such purification is understood to represent the purification of the heart and mind.

Each tea room has a small garden surrounding the guests' entrance. The path through this garden to the tea room leads to a low stone water basin. When the guests have arrived and are waiting, seated at the far side of the garden, the host pours fresh water into the basin. A disciple once asked Rikyu the reason for this, and he answered that the sound and sight of the water gave to the atmosphere a cleansing and refreshing sense.

The garden path itself is said to lead to a world beyond our mundane life. Hence the first act that the host and guests perform in this garden is to purify themselves of the dust of the world. The garden path is called the "dewy ground" (roji), though originally this word may have been written to mean simply "passage" or "path." In a parable in the Lotus Sutra, a father calls his children from a burning house to safety in the roji. The burning house symbolizes the painful existence of ignorance and self-attachment, and practitioners of chanoyu consider their roji to be the place for abandoning the entanglements of this world.

Tranquillity

In general terms, the principle of tranquillity best

expresses the ideal of chanoyu. Amid the bustle of life, chanoyu offers a setting and a discipline for collecting oneself.

The tranquillity of chanoyu, however, is not simply a brief respite from cares, or a relative peacefulness from which to return to our daily responsibilities. Practitioners of chanoyu seek to make this tranquillity the foundation of their lives. The word for "tranquillity," *jaku*, is a Buddhist term that is often used to mean "nirvana," the blowing out of blind passions and the awakening to that which is true and real.

Rikyu had this to say on the nature of chanoyu:

Chanoyu is above all a matter of practicing and realizing the way in accord with the Buddha's teaching. To delight in the splendor of a dwelling or the taste of a sumptuous meal belongs to worldly life. There is shelter enough when the roof does not leak, and food enough when it keeps one from starving. This is the Buddha's teaching and the fundamental intent of chanoyu. The practitioner brings water, gathers firewood, and boils the water. Making tea, he offers it to the

Buddha, serves it to others, and drinks of it himself. He arranged flowers and burns incense. In all of this, he takes for his model the acts of Buddhas and patriarchs.

Here is the essential character of chanoyu as a "way," a path of discipline and practice by which to transcend our false images of ourselves.

A concrete expression of this is the veneration shown toward the calligraphies of Zen monks, which reveal to us the insight of Buddhist awakening. Again to quote Rikyu:

No utensil ranks with the scroll in significance. Contemplating it, both guest and host attain wholeness of mind and realization of the way in *chanoyu-samadhi*. Calligraphies of Zen monks are foremost among scrolls. With veneration for what is written, one savors the virtue of the calligrapher, of practitioners of the way, of the patriarchs.

Just as harmony, respect, and purity not only represent spiritual values, but also manifest themselves in practice, in chanoyu, so tranquillity is both an interior state with concrete effect.

In one of Okakura's most celebrated comments, chanoyu is depicted as the "worship of the Imperfect." In this, he expresses an appreciation of perhaps the most distinctive feature of many treasured tea utensils—their lack of symmetry and formal perfection. The positive value of imperfection is fully evident as well in tea room architecture, which demonstrates the importance of the process of perfecting, which is greater than perfection itself. True beauty, according to Taoist and Zen thought, can be discovered only by one who mentally completes the incomplete. The virility of life and art lie in their possibilities for growth.

The aesthetic appreciation of the incomplete was not original to chanoyu. Even in the classic *Essays in Idleness* (c. 1331), one can find the statement, "In all things whatever, completeness in every detail is undesirable; that which is just left in an unfinished state holds interest."

Okakura's understanding of this preference no doubt arose from his long experience with the artistic traditions of both the East and the West. There are many who might not agree with his idea that the beholder completes the symmetry of, for example, a tea bowl, or that the asymmetrical is appreciated just as it is. But the "worship of the Imperfect" is not simply a formal aesthetic category. "The adoration of the beautiful among the sordid facts of everyday existence," in Okakura's words, is the larger issue, and it is here—in the appreciation of the everyday beyond the calculation and intention of the human mind—that the foundation for aesthetic expression in chanoyu exists.

Much has been said of the aesthetic values of chanoyu— the love of the subdued and austere, most commonly characterized by the term *wabi*. *Wabi* originally suggested an atmosphere of desolation, both in the sense of solitariness and in the sense of the poverty of things. In the long history of various Japanese arts, this sense of *wabi* gradually came to take on a positive meaning, to be recognized for its profound, religious sense.

The tea master Jo'o chose the following poem by Fujiwara Teika to express this sense:

> Gazing long to the shore,
> There are no blossoms
> Or crimson leaves:
> Out at sea's edge, a rush hut
> In autumn dusk.

There is a certain loneliness that the scene evokes—absent the color of the seasons, of spring blossoms or autumn leaves. Perhaps here, in this "imperfection," one awakens most starkly to the truth of our own existence. Only in such essential poverty can we truly perceive the things around us. As Okakura states, "Those who cannot feel the littleness of the great things in themselves are apt to overlook the greatness of little things in others."

Still, the *wabi* of the poem chosen by Jo'o connotes a negativity, whereas this poem by Fujiwara Ietaka, chosen by Rikyu, aspires to it:

> To one who awaits
> Only the cherry's blossoming
> I would show
> Spring in the mountain village,
> Its young herbs amid snow.

Here, *wabi* gives rise to a new awareness. We sense in it the re-emergence of the world with new vitality and meaning.

I once asked my Zen master, Goto Zuigan, about the meaning of the related term, *sabi*. He told me to look at a pond in the temple precincts. I followed his instruction, looking at the waters for a long while, then returned. He asked whether I understood, and I confessed that I did not. He told me to look again.

This time I went to the edge of the pond and selected a large rock on which I could sit in meditation. It was midwinter, and the water's surface was covered with the withered leaves of the lotuses. Suddenly I realized that the flowers had not simply dried up, but that they embodied, in their decomposition, the fullness of life that would emerge again in their natural beauty.

Okakura, speaking of Taoist ideals that pervade chanoyu, states that "the three jewels of life were Pity, Economy, and Modesty." The terms may be old-fashioned now, but they speak of qualities that, in our present world, many of us now seek.

It is now nearly a century since Okakura set down his classic essay. His message is no less compelling, its import perhaps greater. It is, at heart, an admonition that the first and foremost lesson humankind must learn is to live together in harmony, and to respect the achievements of diverse cultures without imposition.

As for myself, it is almost forty years now since I first went to the United States to demonstrate and to talk about the way of tea. Since that time, soon after the war, it has been my conviction that world peace can be achieved starting with the exchange of tea between just two individuals. After more than one hundred trips abroad to dozens of countries in six continents to lecture at universities and organizations, there are now scores of cities around the world where students practice chanoyu.

Still, I am often asked by Japanese who know of my travels how it is that non-Japanese can hope to grasp something that the Japanese themselves find so difficult to understand. I reply that a pine tree is a pine tree, and in whatever land it is planted, it will grow and flourish if supplied with water, air, space, and nourishment. Likewise, human beings require nourishment—both physical and spiritual—and chanoyu can help to provide this nourishment.

The advances of science and technology since Okakura's day, and even since my own youth, have fostered great conveniences in modern life, and widespread prosperity in the developed nations, but they have also brought deep anxiety. The threat of warfare employing weapons of near-inconceivable destructive power, and the steady erosion of the environment, poisoning the air we breathe and the water we drink, are daily realities. It is surely time to look at tea anew, taking the broad perspective that Okakura first proposed, of human culture transcending the boundaries of nations.

Soshitsu Sen XV

October 1989

Social Sciences and History

THE ANATOMY OF DEPENDENCE

Takeo Doi, M.D.
Translated by John Bester

A definitive analysis of *amae*, the indulging, passive love which supports an individual within a group, a key concept in Japanese psychology.

PB, ISBN 0-87011-494-8, 184 pages

THE ANATOMY OF SELF
The Individual Versus Society

Takeo Doi, M.D.
Translated by Mark A. Harbison

A fascinating exploration into the role of the individual in Japan, and Japanese concepts of self-awareness, communication, and relationships.

PB, ISBN 0-87011-902-8, 176 pages

BEYOND NATIONAL BORDERS

Kenichi Ohmae

"[Ohmae is] Japan's only management guru." — *Financial Times*

PB, ISBN 4-7700-1385-X , 144 pages
Available only in Japan.

THE BOOK OF TEA

Kakuzo Okakura
Foreword and Afterword by Soshitsu Sen XV

The seminal text on the meaning and practice of tea, illustrated with eight historic photographs.

PB, ISBN 4-7700-1542-9, 160 pages

THE COMPACT CULTURE
The Japanese Tradition of "Smaller is Better"

O-Young Lee
Translated by Robert N. Huey

A provocative study of Japan's tendency to make the most out of miniaturization, that reveals the essence of Japanese character.

PB, ISBN 4-7700-1543-3, 196 pages

Social Sciences and History

THE JAPANESE NEGOTIATOR
Subtlety and Strategy Beyond Western Logic
Robert M. March

Shows how Japanese negotiate among themselves and examines case studies, providing practical advice for the Western executive.
PB, ISBN 0-87011-962-1, 200 pages

THE JAPANESE THROUGH AMERICAN EYES
Sheila K. Johnson

A revealing look at the images and stereotypes of Japanese produced by American popular culture and media.
PB, ISBN 4-7700-1450-3, 208 pages   Available only in Japan.

JAPAN'S LONGEST DAY
Pacific War Research Society

A detailed account of the day before Japan surrendered, based on eyewitness testimony of the men involved in the decision to surrender.
PB: ISBN 0-87011-422-0, 340 pages

MANGA! MANGA!
The World of Japanese Comics
Frederick L. Schodt
Introduction by Osamu Tezuka

A profusely illustrated and detailed exploration of the world of Japanese comics.
PB, ISBN 0-87011-752-1, 260 pages

NEIGHBORHOOD TOKYO
Theodore C. Bestor

A highly readable glimpse into the everyday lives, commerce, and relationships of some 2,000 neighborhood residents of Tokyo.
PB, ISBN 4-7700-1496-1, 368 pages   Available only in Japan.

THE INLAND SEA
Donald Richie

An award-winning documentary—part travelogue, part intimate diary and meditation—of a journey into the heart of traditional Japan.
PB, ISBN 4-7700-1751, 292 pages

THE THIRD CENTURY
America's Resurgence in the Asian Era

Joel Kotkin and Yoriko Kishimoto

Argues that the U.S. must adopt a realistic and resilient attitude as it faces serious competition from Asia. "Truly powerful public ideas." — *Boston Globe*

PB, ISBN 4-7700-1452-X, 304 pages
Available only in Japan.

THE UNFETTERED MIND
Writings of the Zen Master to the Sword Master

Takuan soho
Translated by William Scott Wilson

Philosophy as useful to today's corporate warriors as it was to seventeenth-century samurai.

PB, ISBN 0-87011-851-X, 104 pages

THE UNSPOKEN WAY
**Haragei, or The Role of Silent Communication
in Japanese Business and Society**

Michihiro Matsumoto

Haragei, a uniquely Japanese concept of communication, affects language, social interaction, and especially business dealings.

PB, ISBN 0-87011-889-7, 152 pages

WOMANSWORD
What Japanese Words Say About Women

Kittredge Cherry

From "cockroach husband" to "daughter-in-a-box," a mix of provocative and entertaining words that collectively tell the story of Japanese women.

PB, ISBN 4-7700-1655-7, 160 pages

WORDS IN CONTEXT
Takao Suzuki
Translation by Akira Miura

One of Japan's foremost linguists explores the complex relationship between language and culture, psychology and lifestyle.

PB, ISBN 0-87011-642-8, 180 pages

Japan's Modern Writers

TUN-HUANG A Novel
Yasushi Inoue
Translated by Jean Oda Moy

An intriguing explanation of one of the great mysteries of western China—how the sacred scrolls of the Sung dynasty were saved from the barbarian tribes of the Hsi-hsia.

PB, ISBN 0-87011-576-6, 216 pages

INTO A BLACK SUN

Takeshi Kaiko
Translated by Cecilia Segawa Seigle

"No other account of Vietnam has been so vivid, so intimate or so moral." —Edmund White, *The New York Times*

PB: ISBN 0-87011-609-6 224 pages, 110 x 182 mm

HOUSE OF SLEEPING BEAUTIES
And Other Stories

Yasunari Kawabata
Translated by Edward Seidensticker
Introduction by Yukio Mishima

Three short stories which center on a lonely protagonist and his peculiar eroticism. Kawabata explores the interplay of fantasy and reality at work on a mind in solitude.

PB, ISBN 0-87011-426-3, 152 pages

THE LAKE

Yasunari Kawabata
Translated by Reiko Tsukimura

By Japan's first nobel laureate for literature. "Seizes the reader's imagination from the first page." —*Village Voice*

PB, ISBN 0-87011-365-8, 168 pages

MONKEY BRAIN SUSHI New Tastes in Japanese Fiction
Edited by Alfred Birnbaum

Fresh, irreverent, and post-Zen, an astounding collection of the brightest and boldest voices in contemporary Japanese fiction.

PB, ISBN 4-7700-1688-3, 312 pages